signature

My God
I Thought You'd Died

My God
I Thought You'd Died

by
Claude Dosdall
with
Joanne Broatch

SEAL BOOKS
McClelland and Stewart-Bantam Limited
Toronto

MY GOD I THOUGHT YOU'D DIED
A Seal Book / September 1986

Grateful acknowledgment is made for permission to reprint two charts from Stress, Psychological Factors and Cancer *by Stephanie Matthews-Simonton, O. Carl Simonton and Jeanne Achterberg. Copyright © 1976 by Cancer Counseling and Research Center. Used by permission of the authors.*

Canadian Cataloguing in Publication Data

Dosdall, Claude.
  My God I thought you'd died

Bibliography: p.
ISBN 0-7704-2120-2

1. Dosdall, Claude.   2. Cancer - Patients -
Biography.   3. Brain - Tumors - Patients -
Biography.   4. Cancer - Psychological aspects.
I. Broatch, Joanne.   II. Title.

RC280.B7D67 1986   362.1'9699481'00924   C86-093500-0

PRINTED IN CANADA

COVER PRINTED IN U. S. A.

KR   0 9 8 7 6 5 4 3 2 1

*With love and admiration
to Moyra White*

Contents

Foreword

This is the story of one man's fight against, and eventual triumph over, a serious brain cancer. It is an unusually honest and open account, describing the impact of a divorce and separation from family, his inability to continue in a job as hospital administrator, his despair at the weakness and partial paralysis caused by the tumor, his constant battle with self-pity. Claude Dosdall, however, fought back. Like the archetypal character in Joseph Campbell's *Hero with a Thousand Faces,* his life has gradually become a search for understanding and meaning, with visits to workshops, lectures, and healers in many traditions, and with an ever-increasing exploration of his own emotional reactions and needs, and of their relationship to his bodily health.

There have been many books describing alternative or additional treatments for cancer. In Dosdall's script there is a refreshing absence of the usual doctrinaire advocacy of any single mode of treatment. Instead, he argues reasonably for cooperative and multifactorial patient/doctor efforts. One can only respect and admire the courage and commitment of his own efforts to help himself. Claude now runs a center in Vancouver, where, for a nominal fee, he helps other cancer patients to help themselves. He works with humility and compassion, and with this book, his example will inspire thousands more.

Dr. Alastair J. Cunningham
Professor of Medical Biophysics
Ontario Cancer Institute
University of Toronto

A man was sentenced to death by the king. But he obtained a reprieve by assuring the king he could teach his majesty's horse to fly within a year. When friends criticized him for such an absurd promise he answered, "Within a year the king may die. Or I may die. Or the horse may die. And in a year, who knows? Maybe the horse will fly."

1

The Horse Can Fly

"MY GOD I THOUGHT YOU HAD died." These were the first words of an acquaintance when we met by chance in 1978 after not having seen each other for over a year. He had known back then that I had an inoperable brain tumor, and his expectations had been, of course, that I would die. And probably soon.

Len's apology, "I just said it without thinking," reflected his social programming. Everyone knows cancer kills. As well, when he had last seen me, I was limping, listing to one side, and dangling my right arm. People don't recover when things have gone that far.

His expectation was that I would die, and he was greatly surprised that I hadn't. My expectation was that I would beat the odds, and I did. What I know now is that if I had had *his* expectation, I would not be alive today writing this book.

Socrates is supposed to have said, "There is no illness of the body apart from the mind." Shamans, medicine men, and witch doctors operate from this principle, deriving power from their abilities to convince patients that they will live (or sometimes, that it is time for them to die). Their rituals are powerful inasmuch as they stimulate the will, or repair the relationships of the patient with the spirit world and with the people in their society, or all three.

I now realize that a most important factor in a person's treatment is the person's own expectation of recovery. That was true for me.

I am a cancer survivor. When I was well, for the first forty years of my life, I paid little attention to health and certainly none to people with cancer. I never expected to become ill; the possibility never crossed my mind.

Then in 1975 when I had just turned forty, my marriage of

3

sixteen years broke up and I began to experience health problems. The right side of my body gradually became paralyzed. I was limping and stumbling because my balance had gone. It was hard to write. I was tired all the time and terribly depressed. I was diagnosed as having Parkinson's disease and later rediagnosed as having a psychosomatic illness. It wasn't until two years later that the doctor discovered the disease that was "all in my head" really *was* all in my head.

In 1977 the same neurologist who had diagnosed me as having an hysterical conversion to the right side found I had an inoperable astrocytoma brain tumor on the left parietal lobe. It was 8 cm by 6.5 cm, larger than an egg, and he told me there was nothing that anyone could do about it. He had no medical treatments to offer. All I could do was live with this time bomb in my head.

So, in part, this book is a personal account of my fight against cancer. It is about hope and despair, faith and doubt, acceptance and denial, knowing and not knowing, peace and chaos, deciding and putting off, beginning and ending. It is not so much about blood tests and CAT scans, chemotherapy and radiation, biopsy and surgery, although I have become familiar with orthodox medical treatments and I do talk about them. It is more about examining my beliefs, trusting my judgment, dealing with my anger and guilt, learning to ask for what I need, and gradually becoming aware of the connection between my mind and my body. And it is especially about deciding finally to get well and to stay well.

It is about the creative and destructive forces in me, the struggle of deciding whether I wanted to live or give up. It is about changing the belief that my health is a matter of luck. It is about the process of gradually taking responsibility both for my life and for the fact that I live with a deadly brain tumor.

I have three reasons for writing this book. First of all, it is important for me to make sense of what went on during these past ten years, to discover the meaning of it all. I know with certainty that my illness was not an accident that just spontaneously began and then mysteriously ended ten years later. I want to put the events in their wider perspective, and see the meaning of the pain, suffering, and confusion in the overall context of my life.

Second, I feel that it will in some way benefit my four children to read about the process I've gone through. They have gone through many parts of it with me, right from the very first when I reviewed my will with them and talked to them about the possibility of my dying. At times they helped me with the treatments I tried, and encouraged me to be positive and to look after myself. At other times we fought and shouted and I know they saw me as moody, frustrating, impossible, and even crazy. Mainly they loved me and cared even when they were bewildered about what they could do. Many times I was unable to feel the love they were offering me then, and I wonder if I can ever show them how much I love them now.

Third, I believe my story will be of use to other people with cancer. I want to present my story as a simple case study and put alongside it what I have learned from more than a hundred other cancer patients I have worked with, most of them considered terminal and medically incurable. I want to explore with the reader what has worked and not worked for me, and what has worked and not worked for others.

Most important, I want to show that not only the events but also the processes, discovering my determination, learning to accept myself and to trust my own judgment, were an important aspect of my healing.

But this book is more than just my story. It is about the things I know with certainty as a result of my ten years of living with cancer. I have come to know the incredible power with which the mind can influence the body. My personal experience has taught me about psychoneuroimmunology. My psyche and emotional self impact directly on my brain and nervous system, and in turn my brain gives messages to my immune system. My immune system keeps me well when it functions well and leaves my body vulnerable to disease when it doesn't.

What I believe and think determines what happens to my physical body. The doctors believed that my chances of getting well were less than 5 percent but I chose to believe that I was the exception. I was able to relish the difficult odds and use this challenge as an opportunity to explore myself in a way that I never would have done otherwise. I have always felt creative and I used this creativity to beat the odds. Although I have experienced hundreds of doubts during these years, I am increasingly convinced that the mind can overcome physical disease.

> I know that knowing myself is the best insurance program for getting well and staying well.
> I know now that I have a personal power that I never before realized.
> I know that I can rely on my own judgment more than I ever thought.
> I know that confronting anything makes it less frightening.
> I know that positive thinking in many cancer patients is only pretending everything is fine.
> I know that wishes are useless.
> I now know cancer demanded that I change my life or die.
> I know that humor is important to survival.
> I know that we are all connected to some higher power.
> I know that what I believe is what I am.
> I know that the first step in knowing is knowing that you don't know.
> And much, much more.

You might wonder how I came to know all this with such great certainty.

To begin, there was absolutely nothing in my life or background that would have suggested my going down this painful path to discovery. I came from Quinton, Saskatchewan, a small prairie village where everyone knew everyone else, almost everyone attended the same church, and people generally had the same views and similar rural occupations. My father was first a farmer, later the owner of a general store, and finally the operator of a grain elevator. My mother stayed home to look after me and my younger brother. My world was safe and secure, the atmosphere conservative and extremely stable. After high school I went to the University of Saskatchewan in Saskatoon, took graduate training in health care and hospital administration at the University of Toronto, and traveled to Cornell University, on scholarship for a summer program with health professionals from around the world.

When I was twenty-five and in my last year of university, I married Doris, whom I had met at the University of Saskatchewan. We settled in Regina and later moved to Vancouver, where I practiced my profession as a hospital administrator and together we raised four children. I was elected a member of the town council. I was a conservative, stable person living in a conservative, stable environment. Change was not part of my reality. My 1970 self would have looked at my present self and called me a nut.

Then suddenly becoming ill in 1975 and being told I had incurable cancer put me in a crisis situation of the highest order. Newly divorced, partially paralyzed, tired all the time, without enough energy to continue my job, and feeling rejected, depressed, and unloved, I struggled to find out about my illness and heal myself. It was only gradually that I realized health was about being self-aware and about watching my thoughts and actions without judging them. I kept a daily record of my actions, my conversations with doctors, and most important, my feelings. These journals, which add up to over five thousand pages, scrawled at first with my partly paralyzed right hand, then later with my left hand and now again with my well-functioning right, provide the material for my story.

Other facts and insights have come from the people who have become part of the Hope Cancer Help Center which I founded six years ago and now direct. They have contributed tremendously to my knowledge of cancer. In addition, through their sensitivity and courage in dealing with their own disease process, they have given me a great respect and appreciation for life.

Curiosity and a determination to get well and stay well have led me to read books on health, cancer, stress, nutrition, exercise, holistic medicine, psychology, philosophy, and anything that might influence beliefs and healing, particularly in relationship to cancer. My search to get well has taken me to doctors and therapists, naturopaths and acupuncturists, psychic healers and therapy groups, seminars and lectures, meditation retreats, metabolic nutritional programs, wheatgrass therapy, megavitamins, biofeedback, and radiation. This book is about all the good things I did, and about all the mistakes I made.

It is about the process of how I got well again and about the things you can do to help yourself get well and stay well.

Nothing makes a man sick sooner than feeling useless, unwanted, unchallenged and unneeded.

Sidney Jourard

adjustors to deal with, a job that kept me away from home all week, and a body that was starting to collapse. When the insurance adjustor told me to nail up the doors and windows of my burned-out house because he wouldn't be responsible for the contents, I couldn't do it myself. The coordination on my right side was gone, and I was constantly hitting my left hand with the hammer. I had to get help. It was all too much.

Finally I told the people in the Government Hospital Planning Department that they had to let me do my work in Vancouver or I would quit. I was good and they needed me, so they agreed. I found a small dark basement suite for Sherry and myself, and there I struggled to do my work and cope with the horrendous task of verifying, justifying, and documenting everything for the insurance adjustors.

Before the fire I had been exhausted and depressed and had had so much trouble writing, that I hadn't paid my bills for three months. The simple act of writing a check with my deteriorating right hand was too much for me to do and the thought that I was too helpless to write my own checks depressed me so that I couldn't bring myself to ask for help. Frustrated and exhausted, I had turned myself over to a doctor in March 1976. A neurologist diagnosed my condition as Parkinson's disease, prescribed L-Dopa, and referred me to a psychiatrist. The psychiatrist looked at my depression and prescribed Elavil. The two incompatible drugs and the whole uncoordinated treatment put even more of a strain on my already distressed mind and body.

Off on the Wrong Track

Finally, in July I took sick leave and was admitted for three weeks to the University of British Columbia's psychiatric clinic.

As director of planning and research of St. Paul's Hospital from 1969 to 1974, I had worked closely with the medical staff at UBC in planning the psychiatric unit and now it felt strange to be there as a patient.

However, I enjoyed the daily group sessions, and especially all the attention I was getting from my friends. While there, my neurologist and my psychiatrist decided that I had been misdiagnosed. I did not have Parkinson's disease: my condition, they decided, was psychosomatic. They called it "hysterical conversion to the right side."

Well, I guess at some level I was pretty hysterical, and since the doctors were both so sure, I believed them. Since the psychiatrist was so definite, I didn't question him. I asked to be put into a six-week outpatient therapy program because I felt it would be a useful way to become more aware of what was going on with me, and to find out why I had this increasing paralysis on my right side. It was the beginning of a ten-month search.

I remember feeling very down on myself at the time. The doctor gave me the impression that my illness was my fault and that all I really had to do was pull myself together and get back to work. Ironically the expression "It's all in your mind" is correct, if taken literally, but my psychiatrist used it as if to say there was really nothing wrong with me. I was frightened, tired, and depressed; the right side of my body wasn't functioning properly, and I felt I was acting like a crybaby. I had no self-esteem, no self-trust, and worse, I wanted to hide my problem because, after all, the experts were telling me there really wasn't one. I felt even my friends had lost interest and respect. Sherry would say, "Dad, don't limp," with a mixture of concern and embarrassment. After all, hadn't the doctors said there was nothing wrong? I felt totally misunderstood.

In September I resigned my job. I simply did not have the energy to do it, and I felt that I needed the little energy I had left to find out why I was doing this to myself. Had I been correctly diagnosed, I would have been eligible for sick benefits of 75 percent of my salary. As it was, I had to depend on the payout from the fire insurance company to support myself. When this ran out, it added an extra burden of financial worries later on.

The continual fatigue and depression, which are symptoms most cancer patients experience (although I did not know it then), did not stop my innate curiosity and my determination to find out why my body was acting this way. Therapists were telling me that the right hand is the hand that reaches out, and that Doris was my right hand; now with Doris gone, I couldn't reach out. On a metaphoric level it made sense, but knowing it didn't help.

By now the paralysis of my right hand and arm had progressed to the point where I could barely keep writing in my journal, a habit that helped me make sense of difficult situations. Now more than ever I needed to do it, but it was only with great effort that I could scrawl half a dozen lines, one letter at a time, resting my arm at the end of every line. I tried dictating but it was not the same. At the same time, I resisted writing with my left hand, partly because it was slow and unreadable, and partly because it signified abandoning my right arm, giving up on it. Eventually, though, I did have to learn to write with my left.

Each month and later each week I recorded the signs of my physical deterioration, as well as my feelings about it. There were so many things that already I could not take for granted. I couldn't brush my teeth, brush my hair, undo the button of my left shirt sleeve, or easily tie my shoelaces. These small things added to my fear, frustration, and anger. I felt helpless, weak, and worthless, and suicide was still coming up as an option. In November I wrote, "Lately I'm so afraid of everything that I just want to stay in bed with the blankets pulled over my head." The fear of being a cripple was always with me. Each time there was something else I couldn't do, I panicked. I think what kept me going were my curiosity about the progress of my paralysis and my constant and continual fantasy of getting back again with Doris.

In December 1976, I went to California for eight weeks and I spent New Year's at Esalen, with the goal of letting go of the psychic pain around Doris, and finding a way to regenerate my right side.

Later in January I decided to try acupuncture with Dr. Hector Prestera in Monterey, California. After the energy had been stimulated by the needles, I usually felt better but only for an hour or so. One day I was so low and sick I felt I was dying, and it seemed I'd never be able to drive the 1,500 miles to get home. Then the next day I received my sixth acupuncture treatment and I felt unbelievably good. I even went hiking that weekend with some friends. Then a woman from Berkeley whom I had met at Esalen rejected me (or so I thought) and my exhaustion returned. My right hand was so bad for several days that I couldn't write at all.

By this time I began to realize how my emotional states directly affected my body and I began consciously to play with focusing on a negative situation in my life, to observe how my body reacted. By focusing on a painful, negative situation I could sometimes bring on a headache in less than fifteen minutes. Conversely, focusing on a positive situation had the opposite effect. I was able to do this a number of times, but somehow it seemed far easier to think about the negatives. At this stage I had had two solid years of negative emotion and it had become an easy habit.

Although acupuncture didn't help in the long term, the experience showed me that energy could be stimulated. I started to ask myself which situations in my life gave me energy and which drained me of energy. I became aware of how blocked emotions block energy channels and cause disease. This and everything else I'd learned in those eight weeks—the concepts of energy, responsibility, healing, mind power, and psychic power—were no longer just interesting and sometimes disturbing ideas. They were possible solutions to my problem.

I started out for home in February showing no signs of improvement, but on the way back two significant things happened almost simultaneously: I made a firm commitment to heal myself, and my unconscious diagnosed my illness as cancer.

Both happened on the same day and are recorded on February 23 and February 24. On the twenty-third I woke up with the clear notion that I would heal myself. In fact, it was more than a notion; it was a firm commitment, a commitment that I now know is all-important for any cancer patient to make. I woke up and heard myself saying out loud, "I'm going to heal myself."

The second thing happened that night. I had a dream that was so powerful I recorded it, dictating on a tape recorder because by this time I could hardly write more than a line or two at a time. One sentence that I dictated on the tape was, "I'm in St. Paul's Hospital for a cancer operation." I remembered the whole dream because it was so vivid and I dictated it all without actually hearing myself say the word "cancer." When I arrived back in Vancouver, and was rediagnosed and told I had cancer, I still did not recall myself dictating the word *cancer*. About three months later when I was looking for a blank tape to use, I found the February tape and played it out of curiosity, to hear the dream again. It was then that I heard myself say, "I'm in St. Paul's Hospital for a *cancer* operation." It has always fascinated me that I could have said it out loud and not have consciously registered it. Also in the dream, a voice said to me, "Meditation is healing and surgery is needless." That part made a difference later when I had to make a decision about having a biopsy.

These two incidents were the first of many messages to

me about the power of the mind and the wisdom of the body, and the connection between the two. I was getting a first small hint that my body could tell me what I wanted to know if only my mind would pay attention to it.

Instilling your life with meaning is the single most important factor in moving towards health.

Dr. Carl Simonton

3
Getting on Track

ARRIVING BACK FROM CALIFOR-
nia and still convinced that my problems were psychosomatic, my loneliness and yearning for love were greater than
ever. My isolation kept me in constant pain and my physical
condition was deteriorating. When I walked, my right leg
limped, jarring my body, and my right shoulder sloped so
much that shirts and jackets sometimes slipped off. I was
now brushing my hair and cleaning my teeth with my left
hand. Cooking was extremely difficult as I had only one
hand with which to hold pots and stir at the same time.
Buttoning a shirt and tying shoes were slow and extremely
frustrating tasks. Fumbling through, I was always reminded
I was on my own with nobody to turn to. But my worst
frustrations involved writing. Someone would phone to give
me a message or a phone number and it took so much time to
write it down. It was embarrassing and exhausting.

In this state I went to see the neurologist again, and he
seemed irritated with me for coming back. He agreed
grudgingly to give me a checkup, and these are his words,
which I wrote laboriously into my journal immediately
afterward: "Just to prove to you it's all in your head, I'll give
you a CAT scan." And of course the subsequent CAT scan
showed that it *was* all in my head: I had an egg-sized tumor
on the left side of my brain.

The cancer diagnosis was a relief. Now I knew I wasn't
crazy. I had an enemy I could see.

On May 9, 1977, I was admitted to St. Paul's Hospital for
a nuclear scan and a four-vessel arteriogram, and I was
introduced to a neurosurgeon, who booked me for a craniotomy the following Monday. It seemed illogical to me that I
should have this biopsy. Two specialists had told me that

there was a 90 percent chance that the tumor was an astrocytoma, a slow-growing malignancy, and that the tumor was inoperable because it was too deep. To me it didn't make sense to add the strain of an anesthetic and an operation to my already overstressed body, just to identify a tumor that we all knew was there. Also, I kept remembering the voice in my dream: "Meditation is healing and surgery is needless."

Against the advice of both the neurologist and the neurosurgeon, I had them discharge me on Saturday without the biopsy.

On the Upswing

It was now 1977, almost two years since my marriage breakup, and in that time I had gradually gotten back in touch with all my children. When Doris first left and the boys went with her, I saw them as having rejected me. But now I was able to see that living on Cortes Island, going from the city back to the land (remember, this was the seventies) was all a wonderful adventure to them. At first I had been so hurt that I refused to see Bub when he came to the city to visit. But now the boys came and went frequently, and I wanted a real home for all of us when they came. So just weeks after my cancer diagnosis I bought a house two blocks up from the beach in the Kitsilano area and made plans to move in and renovate in the fall in spite of my terrible physical condition.

At this time I knew nothing at all about cancer, and once more my curiosity moved me to find out all I could about it and about astrocytoma tumors in particular. When Dr. Carl Simonton and Stephanie Matthews-Simonton were invited to conduct a week-long seminar for the Cold Mountain Institute on Cortes Island in May, I attended and I found a lot for me there.

Carl Simonton is a medical doctor, an oncologist, who has had cancer himself and can speak from his own experiences as well as from theory; Stephanie Matthews-Simonton is a psychotherapist. I found Carl to be straightforward, honest, and not at all patronizing. I could relate to him immediately. The Simontons admitted they didn't have all the answers, but they did have a great deal of experience in dealing with cancer patients and they were willing to share what they had learned. Most of all they addressed the psychological aspect of cancer and the importance of beliefs and corresponding attitudes. I was finding out for myself the power of my own mind, and the effect of my own attitudes and emotions on my body.

My main problem was that I was still trapped in depression and despair over the loss of my relationship with Doris and this blocked a lot of learning. Doris was working at the Cold Mountain Institute during the seminar and I was distracted by her most of the time, even though it had been exactly two years to the month since we had separated. Although I was starting to realize the seriousness of the brain tumor, it still took second place to my great loneliness and yearning to have her back. I was still totally preoccupied with getting her back or (alternatively) getting back at her.

But even with the preoccupation and my depressed mental state, I came away from the workshop with several important insights, and what I did manage to hear proved crucial in regaining my health. I found out that in three and a half years Simonton had treated 175 medically incurable patients. Of these, 130 were still alive after twenty-four months. The 45 who had died had lived an average of twenty months longer than had been expected with their diagnosis. To me, these figures were wonderfully encouraging. I also knew I wanted to do more than just extend my life. I wanted to get well.

I also found out that I was getting rewards from my own

illness: I was getting back at Doris by making her feel guilty, and I was getting a lot of attention from her as well. I had a lot of others paying attention and feeling sorry for me, including myself, and it felt so good to feel sorry for myself. I also became aware, for the first time, of the almost continuous stress I had been under for well over a year; and I realized I had to learn to cope with that stress to get well. I learned how to visualize (to consciously focus on images of things or states I wanted and expected to attain) and began the practice regularly two or three times a day.

Most important of all, I came away from the seminar feeling that I was able to do something to help myself.

The Simonton workshop was available to me three months after my decision to heal myself. I see now this was no accident. The enthusiasm and energy from that one-week seminar carried me through for several months, starting at the workshop, where I was able to write down thirteen pages of notes, in contrast to the letter-by-letter writing I had been doing just before. In June I went to the neurologist and quoted him in my journal: "Objectively you seem about the same. I would have expected you to be worse." He told me to continue to do whatever I was doing, but wasn't interested in hearing about the Simonton seminar.

Something to Live For

I felt that life was getting better and better. I was walking farther, and even started to jog a little. I had the use of my arm again and was writing with my right hand. Again, as an important outcome of the Simonton seminar, I started to set goals. After several months of struggle and the help of a therapist, I found my goals. One day when I was resting after jogging, they came into clear focus in my mind. Set in 1977 these are goals I still value today:

1. I want to explore a wide variety of spiritual paths by reading, studying, and practical experience.
2. I want to develop and deepen my relationship with my children as a family and contribute what I can to their development.
3. I want not so much to be a writer, but to write, particularly about the process I've gone through.
4. I want to work with people in a group workshop setting.
5. I want to explore the limits and potentials of my physical body.
6. I want to be loved and loving.
7. I want to write poetry.

I continued to visualize at least twice and most often three times a day. I was experiencing the truth of Kenneth Pelletier's comment in his book *Mind as Healer, Mind as Slayer*, that "when the hopeless-helpless cycle is altered, there is a chance to engage in self-healing." A brain scan in August showed that the tumor had not grown. I started to pay more attention to my diet, eating more vegetables and fruit and less junk. A notation in my journal from that time is: "I've been getting so much attention lately that I haven't been depressed for quite a while now." I also decided that as long as I had money, I would spend it on exploring any possibility that might work for me. This included going to health conferences in various parts of the country, and accumulating a library related to cancer specifically and healing in general.

It Starts to Work

In January 1978 a comparison of a recent CAT scan with previous ones indicated that the tumor had decreased in size and density. In a period of nine months, without medical treatment, I had made considerable progress.

Actually I didn't need a doctor to tell me. I was feeling better and had more energy, even with the stress of renovating the house, having all four children with me in the mess, and being anxious about money. I still had bouts of longing and depression, but they were shorter and less severe. For the first time in two years I felt I was going up instead of down.

The orthodox treatments for cancer are surgery, radiation, and chemotherapy (which I've heard some people refer to as cutting, burning, and poisoning). It seemed I was managing so far on such simple things as good food, exercise, purpose in my life, attention, some specific stress control exercises, and visualization. In early 1978 I added regular physiotherapy, and a number of vitamin and mineral supplements to my diet.

Unfortunately, changes are difficult and happen very slowly; sometimes it takes years for a man to become convinced of the need to change. It took me years . . . I think for me the most difficult thing was to really want to change.

Don Juan
Journey to Ixtlan

4
A Common Mistake

My health had so improved by the spring of 1978 that I accepted a job offer as a consultant to plan and develop a functional program for a hospital in Vernon, 250 miles northeast of Vancouver. I took it partly to make money but mostly to prove myself again, since I had not worked for one and a half years.

I began commuting to Vernon in March 1978 in an optimistic mood, but on April 20, one month after the job started, I wrote, "I must be careful that this stress I'm experiencing lately doesn't cause a relapse." The job was extremely difficult, and since this was the first time I had worked as a private consultant, I felt there could be no relaxing; if *I* didn't write this report, it wouldn't be written. As well, I was feeling pulled by the hospital politics.

Not Listening

One morning I woke up feeling terrible and the only word I could remember from that night's dream was "squeezed." That is how I felt. I was working long hours, refereeing conflicts, and working in an air-conditioned office with no windows and no natural light. I was incredibly stressed, and on top of all this, I had stopped visualizing; one part of me wanted to play guinea pig to find out what would happen when I stopped visualizing, and another part of me believed that somehow I had started to feel better by some happy accident not related to the visualization at all.

I came back to Vancouver from Vernon every weekend totally drained, and found the house was a mess. The kids had been there by themselves all week and we had different standards of cleanliness. We also had different energy levels. No one met me at the airport so I was once more commuting, alone, constantly fatigued, and feeling no one really cared or understood. A CAT scan in June showed that the tumor had grown and the neurologist pronounced it untreatable. I was going downhill again.

A June journal entry reads, "Feeling so desperate this morning. It would be so nice to have someone here for me. My head is pounding and I'm feeling nauseous. I need someone to help me out but there is nobody. I must somehow get my equilibrium back and think more clearly about how to improve my chances of survival." I'm surprised when I look back at these notations that I forced myself to carry on for another very long month to finish the report.

Downers

That summer Bill, a colleague, died of cancer—I had seen him at work only three weeks before and he had seemed to be his usual self. Soon after, another colleague died of cancer and I started to question whether it really was possible ever to recover from it. I felt I was at the end of the line and for a while I did nothing.

Then on June 19 I went to see the neurologist. I asked directly how much time I had to live and he replied, "It could be as much as five years," but his tone was not hopeful. Two weeks later, I went to see the neurosurgeon. He told me exactly what the neurologist said and I felt they had both given up on me. The neurologist suggested we "wait and see," but "wait and see" made no sense to me. Wait for what? See what? Did I wait with hope and trust to luck? Or more likely, with great anxiety and tremendous fear of the unknown?

That day when I got home, I turned on the radio and heard

Paul Simon singing, "The problems are all inside your head she said to me." I burst out laughing. A cosmic joke was being played on me, and by God, it was great to laugh about it just once.

Willing to Die to Finish the Job

After I finished the hospital report, I had two more job offers. It felt good to be wanted but I decided to collect unemployment insurance rather than accept another job. By then I was barely dragging myself around, and the most I could do with my right arm was keep up my journal. I had another significant dream that August, in which a voice said, "You turned it around once before but you'll never do it again using the same kind of music." The message seemed quite clear, but my question was, what else could I do? I had too little energy or enthusiasm to explore alternatives. I tried going back to the Simonton visualizations but couldn't seem to concentrate and I only did them irregularly and halfheartedly. On August second I wrote, "I have given up. . . . There is nobody or any belief I can hang onto to give me comfort." Then I had a dream in which I was playing cards and had the winning hand, but I didn't turn up my four aces and I lost. Everyone knew the rules but me. Again my subconscious was talking to me, but I couldn't figure out the message.

Now, somewhat reluctantly I started looking at alternative cancer treatments. I dismissed laetrile because I could find only one person who was really positive about it and supposedly cured by it. However, I did find out that all the laetrile treatments also involved vitamin programs, so I contacted an orthomolecular specialist from Calgary who came to Vancouver once a month, and I started taking large dosages of vitamins, minerals, and enzymes.

I went to hear Dr. Hans Selye, the pioneer authority on

stress, and in his lecture he emphasized the importance of exercise in health. We spoke together afterward and he advised me to go to the Montreal Neurological Institute, which he considered the best in the world. Another alternative that made sense to me was immunotherapy but I could not find a doctor who was familiar with the material I had read, and one physician told me flatly, "It's dangerous to play with your immune system."

In spite of all this searching, I did not feel a genuine commitment to getting well again. Some part of me felt like a robot, going through the motions but not believing I had any real alternative to death. In fact, most of my energy was focused on thinking about dying and wrestling with my beliefs about death.

In spite of the dream image of "four aces in the hole," something kept me from playing my cards.

Out of Control

During the autumn of 1978, I was irritated most of the time. I felt uncared for and particularly unloved and must have been very unpleasant to live with. The kids were having a difficult time coping with my emotional swings and one day everything blew apart. I had a physical fight with Bub, my oldest son, which of course I lost, and I got into a huge screaming fight with Sherry. Both of them were going to leave home and never come back. I felt such hatred, anger, and frustration against them and the whole world. "Nobody, including God, gives a damn about me and I hate this fucking world." When I scribbled this across the page of my journal, the page tore. I felt more than ever I had reached my limit of being tired, paralyzed, sick, and always rejected by people when I didn't do as they wanted. My head was splitting. In my visualization the image was one of a tumor that filled the entire left half of my head. I knew it had grown and later brain scans confirmed it. My emotional states seemed completely out of my control.

One day Doris brought me an article from *Psychology Today* that described how depression and emotional outbursts were triggered by various points of pressure on the brain. I knew my tumor must have been causing pressure, but when she showed me the article, I blew up at her. To accept as a fact that my moods, actions, and reactions were the result of the brain tumor would be to admit I was losing control of myself, that my problem now was somapsychic, that my body was affecting my mind. On the one hand, it would feel great to deny responsibility, to blame everything on the tumor and release myself from this whole mess I was in. But on the other hand, to do this would be to acknowledge I had no control at all over my life or emotions. I struggled with this choice for a long time. Finally, I decided to consider the tumor as a factor in, but not an excuse for, my behavior. The crisis with Bub and Sherry was resolved when Bub made the first move with a hug that brought me to tears.

My spring 1979 journal:

"This continuing headache is making me really depressed and I'm so weak I hesitate to walk from one room to the other as it takes too much energy; to go downstairs really drains me. What shall I do? I'm eating well and taking vitamins, I meditate but infrequently and when I do I can't seem to concentrate. I ask my dreams for help, but nothing. There's laetrile or Ann Wigmore's wheatgrass therapy. I've really got myself in a corner. I want to give up and yet I can't give up. I'm thinking an awful lot about my funeral and want my ashes spread in Hadden Park down by the ocean. I've had such good times down in that park—it feels like it's my park. Doug [now 11] is urging me to exercise. I'm too tired but love him for his encouragement. Del doesn't say much but is taking over more around the house. God, I wish I had Doris to talk to at a time like this."

Desperate

It was in this state that I decided to take LSD. Years earlier
I had heard of two California psychotherapists who were
giving LSD to dying patients, and I had actually written
Claude Naranjo, who wrote *The Healing Journey*. I had
heard that Stanislov Grof and Joan Halifax, both respected
psychotherapists, were also working with LSD. Del urged
me not to do it, and I appreciated his love and concern but I
felt this was the only way to get the information I needed to
find out how to deal with "the" brain tumor. (I had stopped
referring to it as "mine" because I thought this acknowl-
edged ownership. If I was going to get rid of it, I should stop
calling it mine.)

So I took acid. My notes show that I felt more spiritual
and closer to God, and although now I do feel the strength
and importance of the spiritual, the feeling did not come
from that trip. Acid did not give me the magic answer.

Up

That spring I read *Getting Well Again,* a new book by Carl
Simonton, Stephanie Matthews-Simonton, and James
Creighton, and I remember feeling elated, taking hope once
more that I could do something for myself. I started getting
serious about the visualizations again and I began a period
of searching seriously for other ways to make myself well.

Down Again

Then an acquaintance who was exactly my age was diagnosed as having a brain tumor, and ten days later, he died. It frightened me and set me back because I had no idea it could happen so fast. I felt as though I were on an emotional yo-yo. Unfocused and unhinged, I had four minor car accidents. I was preoccupied with dying and felt there was little to live for since the kids were beginning to withdraw and most of my friends already had. My anger and frustration, self-pity, and depression were driving everyone away.

Even my eight-month relationship with Robyn, a woman I'd met shortly after being diagnosed, was ending. She was angry because she hadn't found out about my cancer until six months into the relationship. I was angry because as supportive as she was, underneath she really felt I was going to die. And of course, my hope of Doris's return was always between us. No woman, no person could replace Doris.

Without Doris I felt chronically unloved. I felt a life without love was a wasted life. I was also quite aware that love was the ultimate healer, and when I didn't feel loved, how could I heal myself? I had written about these feelings in my journal before but at this time experienced the absolute epitome of feeling unloved. I later saw this as what philosophers and metaphysicians meant when they referred to hell. I was certainly making my own hell.

Exploring Death

Since the issue of death persisted, I decided if I was to die it was time to deliberately put what energy I had into exploring death, because I wanted to die in a conscious and aware manner. I registered for a ten-day retreat on death and dying in Yucca Valley, California, in March 1979, to be conducted by Ram Dass and Stephen Levine. I went there wanting to explore four aspects of my life and I came away with many valuable insights.

First, I wanted to explore my spiritual beliefs. I had often written in my journal that I needed a God to turn to for some reassurance and for unconditional love. I knew at the time that belief systems were only ways of thinking and that they were not reality. I knew that I saw the world through my beliefs, and that these beliefs colored my perception of reality. What I came to realize at the workshop was that there is no reality out there to be colored; that at one level, the only reality is what I see—I create my reality—and that realization gave me a great deal of power.

Second, I wanted to explore the significance of my particular form of cancer. Why did I have a brain tumor, and not lung cancer, or lymphoma? I didn't resolve that question there, but months later at another workshop Jack Schwartz, in the context of a talk, said something I felt aimed right at me: "People with brain tumors feel nobody understands them."

Third, I wanted to explore suicide. While I wasn't contemplating it at the time, I still wanted to know more about suicide as an option. I was reassured by what I found out, that it is very common for people with cancer to consider committing suicide, but it is uncommon for them to do it.

And last, I wanted to find a way to reduce my attachment

to Doris which I now saw as an addiction. After four years of separation, my attachment seemed stronger than ever. I had explored every minute detail of our relationship and became even more attached. About six months before, I had awakened one morning, raging out loud, "Life without Doris is not worth living: I'm willing to die for her." The two constants in my life were the tumor and Doris. No matter what I did, the two remained. I was sure there was a connection but I didn't know what it was or how to find out.

I asked Ram Dass what I could do about my attachment and he talked to me about a "thought form," something I really didn't understand then. He suggested I go to a long meditation retreat and he gave me the names of two teachers he respected, Jack Kornfield and Joseph Goldstein. I was bitterly disappointed with what I perceived to be a nonanswer.

Although Doris supported me in it, some of my friends considered it morbid for me to go to a workshop on death and dying. There is no getting around it; during that week, I experienced an incredible amount of grief and shed a lifetime of tears. Many participants, like myself, were in much physical and psychological pain, and we were encouraged to be open to it, not to resist. One of the psychotherapists in the group said she observed that most people will tolerate the physical pain because it is less severe than facing the situation that causes the psychic pain. But far from being morbid, the obvious and surprising thing about the workshop was the fun and joy the 150 people shared. Although many were ill and some were dying, the atmosphere was anything but depressing. I had heard many times that grieving is positive and healing, but here for the first time I truly experienced it.

Nine Weeks of Hell

That March (1979), on my way home from Yucca Valley, I
began the first month of a two-month wheatgrass treatment.
I had read a book called *How I Cured Myself Naturally with
Wheatgrass,* so in another desperate effort, I went to a now-
defunct institute in Santa Cruz to take the cure. It was a
horrendous process.

For two weeks there and seven weeks at home I took
eighteen ounces of wheatgrass juice a day, both by mouth
and with enemas, and ate only vegetables with no salt,
pepper, or dressing. I gave myself three wheatgrass enemas
daily, with only one hand and one leg functioning properly
and no experience ever before with enemas. I remember
those times in the bathroom, when in weakness and frustration, I would burst into tears. I never cried so much in my
life. I felt so sorry for myself. I could hardly drag myself from
the bathroom to the couch where I would lie for hours,
totally wasted. The chlorophyll smell of a new-mown lawn,
which I normally enjoyed, made me throw up. I wasn't
overweight when I started, but I lost twenty-seven pounds.
This whole venture was one of the biggest mistakes I had
made—before or since.

For me the world is weird because it is stupendous, awesome, mysterious, unfathomable; my interest has been to convince you that you must assume responsibility for being here, in this marvellous world, in this marvellous desert, in this time. I wanted to convince you that you must learn to make every act count. . . .

The lessons of Don Juan, in
Journey to Ixtlan

5
Three Journeys

BACK IN VANCOUVER IN APRIL 1979, I noted in my journal, "Right hand so paralyzed, now eating with my left." All that summer I was feeling alone and lost. I was frightened by what was happening to me and I had no one to share it with, despite the fact that I had had a few short-term relationships with women and that I met with therapists to try and sort things out. I tried talking things over with Doris, but my goal was to find a way we could be together again and her goal was to end it and get rid of the guilt. She was able to get rid of her guilt much faster than I could let go of my fantasies. My predominant feeling was that I was uncared for and unloved, and it was a source of great pain for me.

After I completed the wheatgrass treatment at home, in spite of my weakened physical condition and my intense emotional suffering, I accepted a consulting job in Kelowna, much like the one I had done previously in Vernon. Physically I was still going downhill. Until then, even though my right arm dangled and swung by my side, I could still get it to move, but one night in late August when I tried to turn over in bed, I found I couldn't shift my right arm—it just didn't respond at all. This lasted for less than a minute but it was another indication of the downhill slide. I realized then there was a mile's distance between even the slightest movement and no movement at all.

A Concentration Camp

In September 1979 I took time away from my job to participate in a ten-day meditation retreat that my friend Helen had told me about. She and Doris came with me. Led by Joseph Goldstein, the retreat was held at Cultus Lake, a 1½-hour drive from Vancouver, where the natural setting was as beautiful as the buildings were austere. The retreat was situated right on the water, and we could see the towering mountains on the other side of the lake. But the buildings, which had concrete floors and tin roofs, were unheated—even the meditation hall. Most of the time it was rainy and cold, and we slept six to a room in bunks.

The schedule was as demanding as the austere accommodations. A bell rang at 5:30 A.M. for the first meditation, and at 9:30 P.M. for the last. We had two meals, breakfast at 6:30 A.M. and lunch at 11:30 A.M., with a light tea at 5:30 P.M. Silence was broken once a day when Joseph spoke for one hour in the evening.

After the first full day, especially when the bell rang at 5:30 A.M. the second morning, I was convinced I had to get out of there. I was cold, confused, and in intense physical pain. However, I hadn't come with my own car so I stayed.

There were sixty people there in the gray drizzle, people walking about in complete silence or sitting, huddled in blankets, with eyes lowered. I thought, this must be what a concentration camp is like. We were constantly told to be aware of "intending" because when we are aware of the intention, we act with choice. We were to be conscious of our intention before every small act. You don't do very much this way, but the message over and over again was, "There is nowhere to go and nothing to do."

In the one-hour sitting meditation, we were told to focus only on our breath coming in and out. To do this for one minute was difficult; one hour was agony; and fourteen hours a day of walk, sit, walk, sit was indescribable torture. My back ached, my shoulders ached, my neck ached. At night I told myself I would stay just until the next morning, and then hitchhike home if necessary. On the fourth day we were instructed to begin watching the mind states that arose—to observe the state, label it, and then let it go. The mental states were desire, drowsiness, anger, resentment, boredom, worry, and doubt. I went through them all a thousand times. Joseph suggested that in order to motivate yourself, it is helpful to imagine death looking over your shoulder. That was certainly easy for me to do.

50,000 Thoughts per Day

It amazed me how many thoughts I could have when the goal was not to think. No fantasy could possibly be stranger than fourteen hours of my own thoughts. But the state that arose over and over was one of doubt. Why was I wasting my time here when I could be doing something to get well again? Why was I sitting here experiencing the most excruciating physical and psychic pain ever? Why didn't I leave?

As well, I noticed that my brain's message to my arm was taking longer and longer to reach it. During the night my right arm didn't respond at all and I had to move it with my left when I tried to roll over in bed. I desperately wanted to talk to someone about it, particularly to Doris, who was also at the retreat, but the rules of silence were strictly observed. Everyone kept the rules but I decided to see Joseph and I told him briefly what was happening and asked him to do a healing on me. He replied politely that this was a meditation retreat.

Eventually through the days my mind stilled. I had some insights and I made some good decisions during the ten days. I decided to quit work; I decided to sell my share of the property on Cortes Island; and I decided to see the Philippine psychic healers and pay for the trip with the money from the sale of the property. I decided to stay focused and direct from my inner self whether I lived or died.

I also saw that ever since my divorce I had felt unloved and unlovable, and I realized I may have felt this for most of my life. Doris's leaving had just triggered it. Here, now, I was feeling warmth and care from people I had not even met or spoken to. By the fifth day of the retreat I was enjoying the silence and I realized the pain of the past five years had come not so much from missing communication with Doris, but more from feeling isolated from everyone, even those I saw and worked with every day. I had never before recognized this.

Experiencing Love

On September 11, the last full day of the retreat, Joseph came to me as we were going into the 8 A.M. sitting and asked if I still wanted him to do a healing meditation. I was surprised, but said yes without hesitation. I had no idea what a "healing meditation" was even though I had asked for it, but it was to be one of the most remarkable experiences in my life.

Before the sitting began, Joseph asked me to rise so that the sixty participants could see me clearly. I then sat down in my place at the back of the room and Joseph said, "One of our brothers has a physical ailment and I ask you to focus your attention on him for a few minutes." He waited for quiet, then said, "May Claude receive light, love, and healing energy." He waited for a minute or two, then repeated the invocation. He continued in this way for what must have been fifteen minutes.

It is impossible to describe fully the emotional impact of my hearing those words, especially the word "love." The area around my heart immediately felt warm, as if there were streams of heat radiating from it. This continued for over an hour. My body was shaking and vibrating. Tears were coming and I didn't stop them. I felt as though I were submerged in a warm bath of care and affection and I felt totally accepted for what I was. I can't further describe it except to say that I know it was the direct experience of love. Helen and Doris told me later that they and many others were also crying and they, too, spoke of experiencing this intense love. I sat there for four hours in complete peace and harmony.

I think I had somehow opened my body to all the love that had been there in my life, that I just hadn't been able to accept and experience. Many writers on holistic health speak of the healing power of unconditional love and I know now I have experienced it. For five years I had been writing in my journals about feeling unloved. It had kept me in a state of isolation and despair, and along with this terrible feeling of being unloved, I also had a sense of worthlessness. To this day, while I can still experience rejection and hurt, I never feel the scorching pain of being totally unloved and worthless. Here, where there was no place to go and nothing to do, I was able to experience myself for the first time in a really deep way. If there are crucial points in my healing process, I would choose this as one of the most important.

I've realized since then that the feeling of being unloved is common to many people with cancer. LeShan in *You Can Fight for Your Life* describes the dilemma:

You feel as if there are only two possible roads for you in life and you have to choose one of them. The first road is being yourself and expressing yourself as you feel at the moment. It's spontaneous and emotional and warm and loving; and letting others see who you are and how you feel. But you are sure that if you do this, everyone will withdraw from you and reject you and you will be all alone. The second road is to mind your manners and always do exactly what is expected of you, and conform to the wishes of the world. Never to express yourself freely, but always be conscious of others' wishes and expectations. If you follow this second road, people will accept you. But since nobody will know how you feel or who you are, they won't be loving you but a mask, and so you will be just as much alone really, as if you had taken the first road.

I had been on the second road, and now I was off: I wasted much less energy from then on, because I could simply be myself. Physically I was at my lowest point—but mentally and emotionally, I was on the way up.

However, mental and emotional healing precede physical healing, by quite a long period of time sometimes, so the winter was still bad for me. I had constant pain across my shoulders and neck, and my right arm was always tensed in spasm; I just could not relax it. In October I had another car accident because I wasn't paying attention. And I knew accidents were no accident.

I couldn't accept the constant image I had of myself as a cripple and I hated losing my independence. I couldn't accept my clumsiness. My arm swung around, knocking things over. Once it swung into a Skilsaw and I could have lost several fingers, but got away with a few stitches.

My accidents and clumsiness were the result of total frustration and anger, and a journal entry from that time reads: "Total disgust with myself."

To the Philippines

On December 27, 1979, following through on a decision I had made at the meditation retreat, I boarded a Northwest Orient 747 bound for Manila. In another last-ditch effort I was going to the Philippines to see the psychic healers.

The trip itself was a mixture of fun and frustration, pain and healing. Doris came with me, as I could never have managed alone. We stopped to visit friends in Hawaii and also spent time in Hong Kong. That was the fun. The frustration came from my still wanting to be with Doris and still wanting her sexually, which caused more than one major argument. Once she almost flew home before we reached the Philippines.

By 8:30 A.M. Monday, the day after we landed in Manila, I was at Alex Orbito's place, 9 Maryland Street. This name and address was given to me by Dr. Lee Pulos, a Vancouver psychologist who had made several trips to the Philippines to study psychic healers. He had given us the names of five or six he had confidence in, and, more importantly, specific directions to find them. There were no addresses since almost all the healers live in small villages or on farms on unnamed roads, and very few are in the cities. Although I had read two books on healers, I still didn't really know what to expect.

We were greeted by Dr. Rosario, who spoke English. She had been cured of a serious illness by Alex Orbito and now she was acting as his assistant.

There were about twenty people, all natives, quietly waiting in a small chapel with wooden benches and chairs. A small, glassed-in room at the front held a bare wooden table and a crucifix, and Alex Orbito, Dr. Rosario, and two other assistants stood in that area. Orbito spoke briefly to us about his role as a channel for spiritual power, and about the need for us to be positive.

When it was my turn, Dr. Rosario explained my case to Alex. I lay on the bare wooden table on my back, and he worked on the left side of my neck taking out what looked like bloody clots and a small piece of tissue. I could feel the blood running down my chin. I was on the table no more than two or three minutes, and felt a slight pain from the pressure of his hands, but that was all. Doris stood beside me and took pictures. Orbito also gave me some herbal remedy, which he said would improve the blood circulation in the brain, and said next time he'd work on the actual area of my tumor.

After the treatment I felt noticeably weaker, especially in my right leg. Once back at the hotel I slept for fourteen hours.

Doris and I went to a lecture the next evening to learn about psychic healers. The healers believe the body cells are held together by the spirit and the healer can *allow* the cells to move apart so he can put his hand into the body and remove the diseased cells (but not tissue). The healer sees the body in terms of dark and light areas (I imagined it like an X-ray film), and he puts his hands into the dark spots, where, like magnets, they attract the diseased cells, which he removes. Orbito stated he had an obligation to help people, but only God could give guarantees. He suggested that for self-healing we visualize that the light in our minds would put out the darkness in our bodies, but he didn't elaborate.

From my reading I knew that spiritual healers believe that man is both a spiritual being and a physical being and this spiritual life force in us heals the physical body. They believe that when you heal the spiritual being, the physical healing will follow, and they see themselves as channels of power to aid that healing.

When I went for my third treatment, Orbito took something out of my right shoulder and suggested another five treatments but I didn't go back. The crowds and heat in Manila were exhausting me, so I decided to go three hours north to Urdaneta, Prangasinan, the area where most healers work, to visit Juanito Flores.

When we arrived at 9:15 A.M., the chapel was empty and an old lady told us that Juanito was still working in the rice fields. Farmers go to the fields around 5:30 A.M. and then stop at noon because of the heat. The chapel was small and shabby, with peeling paint, a cement floor, and at the front, a sacred area with the usual wooden table. It was cool and peaceful inside the chapel and occasionally a chicken would wander in. The pleasant odor of a wood fire in the yard drifted in, and out among the chickens, ducks, dogs, and cats, a water buffalo stood chewing its cud. The lush green of the trees and palms was very soothing.

After three hours, Flores came in, looking very young, strong, and healthy. I was told he had begun healing when he was fourteen years old and was now thirty-eight. The service was opened by a woman who spoke alternately in English and Tagalog and the dozen or so people who had been waiting now came up as Flores called their names.

Challenging My Beliefs

First Flores gave everyone spiritual injections. There was concentration, compassion, and some humor around them and a definite flare for showmanship by Flores. Flores reached into the air for an imaginary hypodermic needle, which he placed against the Bible, as if to "charge" it. Then he aimed at the patient by pointing his finger, as if giving a shot, and this felt like a pin prick or a mild electric shock. Occasionally there would even be a few drops of blood, but he never touched the patient and usually stood at least three feet away. We unmistakably felt the pin pricks of these injections and people who had had them before winced in anticipation of what they would feel. Experts who have studied the healers explain these spiritual "shots" as a kind of psychokinesis.

He pulled teeth from two patients using only his hands and it seemed to be painless to them. He also did some spinal adjustment on a girl of about fourteen who had a malformed leg. When I was finally called, I felt anxious and wondered how I could tell him about the tumor when he didn't speak English.

He took an ordinary piece of blank paper and held it in front of me, looking through it at me as though he were x-raying me. He went up and down my body, stopping at the left side of my head, right where the tumor was, and then motioned me to lie face down on the bare wooden table with a Bible under my forehead. Then, just as he was ready to start, I felt his head fall against me. He had collapsed.

We found out later that a visitor who had gone up on the platform uninvited to get a closer look had broken Flores's trance by crossing between him and his spiritual healing banner.

Flores left to rest and returned in a half hour, and after calling several others up, he motioned to me. Doris, who was standing on the right side at the head of the table, saw him put his fingers in my skull, and after working for two or three minutes, he slipped out a piece of flesh about the size of a chicken egg. (My neurosurgeon had described my tumor as being "like a chicken egg.") Doris then saw the skin closed, the blood wiped up—it was over. I had felt the blood running along my forehead and nose but I felt no pain. When I got up, Flores showed me the tumor and then threw it into a bucket. I went back to my bench and a few native people came up beaming to shake my hand.

I went to see other healers as well, such as Jopefina Sison,

Marcelino Asuigui, and Tony Agpaoa. They were some of the better known healers who had been written about after visits from German, Swiss, Japanese, and American doctors. Agpaoa, probably the most well known to the outside world, worked in a large clinic/hotel arrangement in Baguio City. He was seeing hundreds of Americans and Europeans a day, most flown in by tour companies, and local rumor was that he was losing his psychic powers by commercializing them. We spent little time in the cities, but stayed mostly near the healers who felt right for me.

We stayed at Urdaneta near Flores, and there we met another healer, Rosita Agaed, a loving, compassionate woman who became our friend. She spoke limited English but her daughter translated. We first met her in a regular healing session and then later visited her and her various relatives, who sat around her chapel in the evenings. After dinner, as we all sat talking and laughing, she would "operate," mostly on my right arm, usually taking out what looked like blood clots, then massaging my arm.

How my reality had changed in only two weeks, since the time when "operations" had seemed so threatening and so awesome! Now while she was operating I paid hardly any attention. I just sat and talked about Vancouver, my children, and my life in Canada.

The term *"psychic operation"* is misleading to Western minds. Actually, it is a healing. A body that is lifeless and ill needs the continuous energy a healer can provide while in a trance state. This is why it is important to work with a healer one-to-one over an extended period of time. Spiritual healers see man as a spiritual being as well as a physical one, the spiritual being providing the internal life force within us. Stimulating this energy on a spiritual level initiates the healing of the physical body.

Most importantly, the healer does not do the actual healing but reinforces or supplements a person's own ability to heal himself. This is a principle accepted by most authorities on paranormal healing and it was making more and more sense to me. To me it meant we do have an innate healing power, which, when we're ill, has failed to function. However, with the right combination of factors, support, and stimulation, our own basic system will heal us.

We stayed in Urdaneta until Saturday and I was prepared to stay longer if Flores "operated" again, as this meant to me that I would need more treatments.

He again held the paper in front of my body as if x-raying me, taking a long time but turning finally to Doris to tell her she should massage my head, indicating that while I was not well yet, I would get well again. I took this to mean the tumor was gone. That day, January 19, I wrote in my journal: "The good news from Juanito had us both crying. It was a moving time and most of the people in the chapel responded in an emotional way." I wrote, "It feels so complete that now I can go home although I know it will require determination and persistence to regain the use of my arm and leg." The next day we boarded a plane for Tokyo and then home.

Back from the Philippines I was no better physically but I was optimistic. I arrived home January 30, 1980, the day before my forty-fifth birthday. My kids had organized a big birthday party for me and I was touched. They had gone to a great deal of trouble to find names and phone numbers of my friends, many of whom they'd heard me refer to only by a first name. It was a wonderful party and a loving home-coming.

To Cold Mountain

Two weeks later, I went to Cold Mountain, a human growth center on Cortes Island—similar to Esalen in California. I registered for the Phase Program directed by Drs. Bennett

Wong and Jock McKeen. It was made up of two one-month group sessions with a month's recess between them. In the first month we would concentrate on exploring the self and in the second month we were to investigate ourselves in relationship to others. My aim was to get my spiritual and emotional selves together.

This was an experience I had wanted for about five years, and now because of my condition, I was giving myself permission to do it. I felt I had little to lose. People who find they have terminal cancer often begin doing things they've always wanted to do. Often it is travel. This is an interesting phenomenon because people prone to cancer have some personality traits in common and one is that they don't do things for *themselves* until death appears around the corner. Life for the cancer-prone usually consists of doing things for others, and until then, I guess I was no exception. (During the program I decided to concentrate on doing what I wanted and at the end of the program I was voted the most self-indulgent member of the group. Success!!)

While at Cold Mountain, the movement in my right leg became more restricted and twice didn't respond at all to my brain's command to move. My "crippledness" was always foremost in my mind and now it was even in my dreams. My journal entry for April 15 reads:

"Last night's dream—'I'm in London walking with a woman friend in a narrow stone passage when I need to go to the bathroom. I notice there is a bathroom for cripples on the third floor and decide to use it. I go in and there are attendants to help the cripples.' . . . I wake up, have to go to the bathroom. I stumble going up the stairs and burst out crying."

Still a Victim

Through the program I discovered many things about myself. I realized what a "blamer" I was, and as a blamer I was always a victim. I discovered how needy I was. Acknowledging this made me feel freer to ask *directly* for what I wanted. I learned that needs have a drive and energy of their own and always try to fulfill themselves, and when I didn't acknowledge them they were filled in indirect ways, illness being one of them. Carl Simonton had pointed this out in his seminar and finally, I got it: Illness was my way of getting essential needs met in an indirect way.

I also recognized that my big need ever since I was a child was to be understood. This didn't necessarily mean needing someone to agree with me, but it meant needing someone to really see me for what I was, without my masks, and understand and love me for who I was, not for what they wanted me to be. Bennett Wong helped me see this more clearly. I also realized that Doris had understood me in a way no one else ever had in my life. Ironically, seeing this somehow helped reduce my attachment to her. It was to be a matter of only six months after recognizing this that both Doris and the tumor ceased to be the main preoccupations of my life.

But the doing was not as easy as the telling of it. I had a hard time during the program because physically I was doing badly and I felt isolated from the other participants a lot of the time. But several good things came out of the hard times.

Discovering My Anger

One good thing was that I tapped into an incredible amount of my anger there. I was angry that I was a cripple, angry that I was unattractive, angry at Doris, angry at just about everything. Normally I was very reserved because as a Catholic and a hardworking prairie boy, I had learned that I shouldn't abandon myself to my emotions. I had read somewhere that cancer is imploded anger and I realized this anger I was holding in could kill me. But the fear of letting it out was even more threatening.

I had my first seizure during the program and I see that seizure as a reflection of that huge anger. On the day of the first seizure I was up in the library writing in my journal. (By now I was writing quite well with my left hand.) I had just written, "I'm by myself again and I'm getting no attention from the group, so I've withdrawn. Nobody comes up to me." I closed my journal and walked over to the stairs leading down to the living room, where most of the group was sitting. I fell down the stairs in full view of twenty people.

I felt tremendous anger, frustration, and rage. I remember intending to jump up and leave. I wouldn't be a cripple in front of all these people. I was lying on my left arm with my right arm stretched out but I had no sense of where my right arm was. I tried to jump up but couldn't. My rage was overwhelming. I wanted to hit out and scream but I was completely paralyzed and the physical pain was excruciating. The tension between wanting to move and not being able to move increased the pain and paralysis. The more I tried to raise myself, the greater the intensity of the pain. I couldn't move and couldn't utter a word but was conscious of everything going on. One of the doctors and two members of the group lifted me and put me on the couch.

It didn't take me long to recognize that I now had everyone's undivided attention and to connect that to the feelings of rejection and exclusion I had just been writing about.

Bennett later told me that it was unusual for someone to remain completely conscious during such a seizure. I think this came from a fear I've always had of losing consciousness, or losing control. Staying conscious through this and through the two seizures I had later enabled me to find a way to control them without using medication. I could do this by absolutely relaxing myself and letting go of the frustration and the anger before my body was frozen by them. I also learned to recognize the anger and release it instead of bottling it up.

Toward the end of the second month of the program I was sitting outside one night listening to the ocean washing against the rocks and I asked myself why I was dying. I wondered why, since I was dying, I was still struggling so hard to have my needs met and why, since I was dying, I was still worrying about my image. It didn't make sense. I realized then that although I was dying what other people thought still did matter to me.

I also saw I had been given many precious gifts in my life, especially since the three "crises"—turning forty, losing Doris, and having cancer. In some cosmically funny way maybe my life had begun at forty. The greatest gift for me, without a doubt, was the overwhelming unconditional love I experienced at the meditation retreat. R. D. Laing sums it up for me when he says, "The fact of life for me is love: whether life is worth living depends for me on whether there is love in my life." I recognized the amount of love and deep caring there was in my life.

I felt it intensely at that moment but knew I still seemed to forget it so easily and so often.

Let Go or Die

Another thing that happened during the program is that I started to see how important it was to let go of Doris. I had always felt that I would die if I had to let her go, but I was beginning to see that if I didn't let her go, I really would die. I know now that it is common in profiles of cancer patients that they form a symbiotic relationship with someone—often their mother—early in life. That "someone" does not fully meet their needs, so when they get older, they find a someone who really does meet their needs, and they put all their eggs in that basket. This was true for me.

I never shared anything important with anyone but Doris, so when she left me, there was absolutely no one else in the world. It didn't matter how many people were willing to talk to me or be with me, that person, Doris, was the *only* one I wanted.

Finally I realized that I had a choice—either let go of Doris or die. I guess I had had a sense of that choice for a long time, but now it was absolutely clear. I was accepting the fact that I could—must—survive without her. I remember a dream I had recorded, where I had written down the words, "I'd rather be tortured than be abandoned by Doris," and it seemed that ultimately both things happened. It seemed that the story of my illness so far was trying to deal with that lost relationship. Lawrence LeShan, in *You Can Fight for Your Life*, talks about the typical cancer patient: "Life is dominated by a problem he must solve, but cannot. The failure of [the] life force is usually connected with this unsolved problem and it's usually due to a relationship." To that I could only say, *amen*. Again it was one of those things in my life that was clearly easier to see than to do, but even the acceptance of the idea made a significant difference that spring and summer.

When I finished the program at the end of April, I reflected on my past four years. It seemed I had been searching for the "magic pill," even though I had heard very early on in my search, from Carl Simonton, that there wasn't one. Whenever I was focused on chasing the emotional or spiritual clues, somewhere I would be reminded that it was in the physical that I would find the answer. Then when I redirected myself toward putting together the physical clues, I bumped into the importance of the spiritual and emotional. In spite of my stubbornness, which made me a slow learner in some respects, I was starting to get the message: Physical and emotional healing go together and the emotional healing must come first.

At the end of April, when the program was over, my body was getting worse but my mind was becoming clearer. I now sensed that when I got myself together emotionally, I would be able to make it physically, and one depended on the other.

Throughout the two-month program Jock had been giving me regular acupuncture treatments and temporarily stimulated the energy so I could raise my right arm above my shoulder for as long as a minute. But both he and Ben urged me to see the neurologist to further explore my medical options.

When a man decides to do something he must go all the way—he must take responsibility for what he does. No matter what he does he must know first why he is doing it, and then he must proceed with his actions without having doubts or remorse about them.

The lessons of Don Juan, in
Journey to Ixtlan

6

The Medical Option

A YEAR AND A HALF BEFORE, IN 1978, the neurologist had ruled out both chemotherapy and radiation. He told me, "The tumor is slow-growing so radiation would work very slowly in shrinking it. At the same time it could destroy other brain cells and cause damage beyond any value you'd obtain. If the tumor was very malignant, radiation would be more effective." After that visit I had written, "No medical treatment available for me." He had sounded so definite that I did not seriously question this again. The neurosurgeon had also said basically the same thing, he and the neurologist supporting each other's opinion.

Now, in May 1980, the neurosurgeon told me the tumor was growing and referred me to the Cancer Clinic. I became patient 80-3937, the 3,937th new cancer patient to go to the clinic in 1980. I was given a little card with the number on it for my appointments.

The first thing I did was try to find out what my life expectancy would be with treatment and without treatment. I annoyed a number of people, and I never did get an answer. By this time I was weary and wary of doctors and I questioned anything they said. They felt I was a real nuisance. The first time I went to the Cancer Clinic was in June 1980. The doctor assigned to me was Dr. D. I spent over three hours at the clinic, ten minutes filling out forms, two hours and forty minutes waiting, and ten minutes with Dr. D. He urged me to have a biopsy so he would have more information, assuming my neurologist had informed me of the risks. He hadn't.

Dr. D. gave me the information about biopsy and radiation in a very straightforward way that I appreciated. With radiation I would lose my hair, but not permanently. My life expectancy would not likely be over five years but he would not be more specific. When I asked, he admitted there would be deterioration of the brain. There was a 90 percent chance the tumor was an astrocytoma, a slow-growing grade one or two, but it could change to a fast-growing tumor. He talked about the exponential growth of tumors and urged me to start radiation as soon as possible.

I felt confused and tense about what to do—radiation? or biopsy? or neither? My trust of doctors was, by this time, low. Dr. Anzarul now said radiation was my only option; Dr. Hayward Rogers said it was up to me. I was not used to this kind of approach from a doctor so I assumed he was uninterested. However, Rogers later called me at home and talked for half an hour about cancer and health. He also explained to me why hyperthermia, used to stimulate the immune system, would not work for a brain tumor.

By now the doctor at the Cancer Clinic was pushing me to say "yes" to radiation so he could get on with it but I was still gathering evidence. I went to Seattle in July to hear Carl Simonton and to talk to him. Like Dr. Rogers, he said the decision was up to me, although he reminded me that the program at his center in Texas was an adjunct to, not a substitute for, conventional medical treatment.

A Tough Decision

It was August now and I had been trying to decide since June. I saw this as a life-or-death matter. If the tumor didn't respond to the radiation, I would harm my body even further and I was concerned about what it would do to my brain, my memory, my eyesight. Already the oncologist and the neurosurgeon were amazed that with such a massive tumor my symptoms weren't greater.

I decided to consult Andrew Feldmar, a therapist with whom I had worked in the past. He told me that the ambivalence in my life was causing extreme stress. Well, I already knew that. He pointed out how dramatic a brain tumor was; this I also knew. It made a large impression on my friends but the novelty was rapidly wearing off. He pointed out how fascinated I was with exploring myself and how the tumor had given me a reason to go on a full-time exploration. Yes, I recognized that and knew how much a part of me really enjoyed it. He emphasized I'd have to find something in my life that was more interesting and intense than the tumor before I'd give it up and I agreed.

But none of this helped me decide whether or not to go ahead with radiation.

I decided to check out the credentials of Dr. X*. and the B.C. Cancer Clinic. It wasn't easy, since people seldom do this and there is no system set up for it. However, I did contact a woman, also with a brain tumor, who had explored every medical option available on the West Coast, down through to California. She had accepted Dr. X. and felt that the B.C. Cancer Clinic was excellent in facilities and weak only in its unwillingness to provide psychological support and alternative adjuncts to the conventional treatments.

Finally, I decided. On August 4, 1980, I wrote:

"Made decision to go with radiation. I wish I felt more certain of it, but now that I've made it I intend to quit agonizing and do everything possible in supporting myself and cooperating with this treatment. The stakes are high—my life. I've got to be positive. I will not allow a biopsy—too risky for the possible rewards."

I did not want anesthesia nor did I want a hole drilled in my head, and since Dr. X. was 90 percent certain it was an astrocytoma, as far as I could determine, the radiation treatment would be the same no matter what a biopsy showed.

The doctor was frustrated but reluctantly agreed to

*Dr. X. is a pseudonym.

radiate without the biopsy. He was especially annoyed because he and the neurologists had recommended radiation in June, and here it was August already. Although I appreciated his directness, he did not appreciate my caution and our relationship was prickly, at best.

It didn't improve when I postponed the radiation one more time to go to a ten-day meditation retreat with Jack Kornfield, in early September.

I was preparing myself for the radiation, doing everything I could to minimize the harmful effects, and maximize the positive effects. I learned biofeedback relaxation techniques. I took moderate doses of Vitamin C (3 grams) and 50,000 grams of Vitamin A, and drank chaparral tea. I knew I would be tired, so I organized my life with that in mind. I worked with Andrew Feldmar to discuss a specific visualization to use during radiation itself. I decided to visualize the tumor being smashed by millions of high-energy bullets. As it turned out, the whirr of the machine in Cobalt Room One further symbolized this high energy for me. I saw radiation as a friend, breaking up the tumor. By doing this I would be using the Simonton approach, cooperating with the treatment.

I started and adhered to a regular exercise program. In July, Simonton had reminded me that "exercise stimulates the immune system and it seems to be one of the best things for depression." I played racquetball with my left hand, stumbling a lot and sometimes hitting my dangling right arm with the racquet, but I persisted, thanks to the encouragement of the two friends I played with.

My journal entry for September 10, 1980, reads: "First radiation treatment; no adverse effect or tiredness. I asked the doctor what I could do to assist myself during the radiation. 'Nothing,' he answered. I don't think he really knew what I was asking."

The journal entry for September 17, 1980, says: "The doctor is such an asshole. Each time I go to see him I wait for more than two hours. It makes me feel like I don't count,

I'm not important, and everything is for his convenience. At first I thought my irritation was due to the radiation but now I know it's due to him."

The next week, after waiting again I exploded. I told the technician I was leaving and I wanted a new doctor. The more she patronized me and tried to calm me down, the more frustrated and angry I became. I stood in the middle of the waiting room waving my one good arm, telling the dozen waiting patients what a bunch of sheep they were. I told them how, by being submissive and passive, we just encouraged the doctors to keep us waiting. Quite a few agreed with me and the room became charged with energy. That was before my fifth treatment. After that I never had to wait longer than twenty minutes.

During those times in the waiting room even I was amazed at the stories of misdiagnosis, the stories of endless waiting, and the amount of confusion about treatment. In most cases, patients passively accepted what was happening in a sickeningly stoic way.

From my journal: "Feeling rejected again by Doris in particular and women in general, and now by treatment number fourteen my hair is gone and I feel old and ugly." Generally, though, I was very positive and other than having minor nausea the only side effect I experienced was extreme fatigue. I would drive home after the treatment, and fall asleep in the car outside the house. No one had warned me that the exhaustion would be cumulative. I slept at least twelve hours a night.

During the course of the treatment I had a blood test once a week to check the white cell count. White cells are destroyed by radiation, and if the white count drops too low, the treatment is discontinued until the count comes back up. When it is low, it is a sign the immune system is dangerously weak and you could die from contracting a common cold. Both radiation and chemotherapy treatments are generally considered more effective if they aren't interrupted, so on September 19 when I found this out, I started to keep a record. On that day my white cell count was 4.75. After fourteen treatments the count had dropped to 3.6, on the low side of normal, and I didn't want it to drop any farther for fear the clinic would interrupt my treatment. I decided to visualize several times a day my bone marrow manufacturing white blood cells. After six more treatments (by treatment twenty), the count was expected to have dropped below the 3.6 of the previous week. It was up to 5.5. By the time I had finished the twenty-five treatments, the count was 7.0. I was elated. The visualizations had worked. (The effectiveness of increasing white blood cells through visualization has since been verified in studies with medical students at the University of Pennsylvania.)

While the doctor, whom I now called by his first name, and I still often disagreed, by the end of my treatment we had established a good connection.

During the time of radiation I kept feeling that the tumor was not disappearing but rather that it was being "nullified," which meant it was still there, but inactive. A CAT scan in November confirmed this and also showed the oblong tumor had decreased from 8 cm to 6 cm in length and from 6 cm to 4.5 cm in width. It was still a very large tumor but this 2 cm represented a 50 percent decrease in tumor mass and this was what was needed to free up my right side. By treatment number twenty-three (two more to go), I lifted my right arm above my head. Ecstasy—the first sign of improvement. Two days later I was able to open my right fist, rather than having to pry it open with my left hand.

The night before the last treatment, I had a dream whose theme was "completion," a confirmation of what I felt. October 13, 1980, was Thanksgiving Monday and I recorded this poem of thanks in my journal:

Thank you, God, or should I say, thank you, Claude
Whoever or whatever, thank you.
I feel grateful, fortunate, and appreciative
And want to thank you on this special day

That has culminated in good things for me.
Thank you for the pleasure of getting up and standing up
Without losing my balance and falling over,
Without my leg collapsing and my arm aching,
Without the constant thought that tomorrow will be worse
And the day will end with me a helpless cripple.

Thank you for family and friends,
For the intimacy and love I have experienced.
A soul that has not experienced love is a cold, sterile shell
So thank you for the love that this day brings.

Thank you for my body's peace and harmony
A respite from the years of turmoil and fear
To relax and feel, whatever, is okay.
To accept myself without denying faults
Has a harmony and peacefulness that is sweet
Is sweet as the mellow sun warming this autumn day.

So thank you, God, for Thanksgiving 1980.

Study indicates cancer toll rise

GENEVA (AP) — Cancer deaths in developed nations increased 55 percent for men and 40 percent for women during the 20-year period ending in 1980, the World Health Organization said Friday.

WHO said lung-cancer deaths increased the most, going from 578,000 a year among men in 1960 to 898,000 in 1980. About 66,000 women died of lung cancer in 1980 compared to 22,000 in 1960.

Most of the countries surveyed were in Europe, but the study also included the United States, Canada, Australia and Japan.

April 27, 1985

The research required for the challenge of eliminating cancer is expensive. Because of research, the statistics regarding cancer survival rates are improving steadily.

Fund-raising brochure, *Canadian Cancer Society*, 1985.

7
Reflections

On My Radiation Treatments

I IMAGINE THERE ARE MANY who feel that radiation was the treatment that "cured" my cancer, that I had wasted three years doing all kinds of useless and expensive things when I could and should have had radiation to begin with.

None of the doctors had suggested radiation as a possibility at first, and even if they had, I don't think it would have worked in 1978 or 1979, because I wasn't ready. And I don't think that it was radiation alone that began my ultimate return to health. I think the radiation worked because I was ready for it to work and because it was working in conjunction with several other things. In fact, I know that radiation has not been effective for many other people with brain tumors.

Why are the side effects so severe for some, when they weren't for me? Why is it that often the tumor doesn't shrink? Why, when the tumor does shrink, does it often grow again in as little as six months? I believe the answers to these questions may be determined by whether or not the patient is prepared enough so that the radiation *can* work.

Cancer is a multifactorial disease, like many modern diseases. Whatever several factors cause it, the one that is the proverbial last straw is the one that makes the final break in the immune system so that the renegade body cells begin to multiply. I believe the cure must also be multifactorial, and of the several factors that worked to arrest and shrink my tumor, radiation was "the final straw" that completed the recovery of my immune system.

It does not make sense to me that doctors will use one or a

combination of the three conventional treatments—radiation, chemotherapy, and surgery—without first working to strengthen the already weakened immune system, as I did. It seems absurd to me that they will intrude on a body already weakened by these cancerous cells, without somehow trying to strengthen the normal cells.

From my reading, my personal experience, and the experience of the members of Hope, I am convinced that the radiation worked for me because I was physically, mentally, and emotionally ready; that I had strengthened myself in every possible way. For my body I had added extra vitamin C because of the extra stress of the radiation. I was as conscientious and as consistent as possible with diet and exercise.

I was especially ready mentally, and as well as the regular visualizations that I did three times a day, I had devised one to use while I was in Cobalt Room 1 during the actual treatment. I visualized the attacking rays as my friends. As well, when my blood count went down, I visualized my bone marrow as a huge factory turning out billions of white blood cells. With the help of a local doctor and a biofeedback machine, I learned to relax myself totally before and during treatment.

Also, even while I was playing out my dramas of depression and suicide, at a much deeper level I was still committed to living. Every day I was still repeating two affirmations, telling myself, "I'm happy, healing, and healthy" and "My body has the ability to heal itself," programming myself to get well. I have often thought that while the drama I played out was almost a melodrama of rejection, despair, and suicide, it was infinitely healthier than the other dramas that I see more frequently played out. In these the person with cancer is "fine," "taking it well," and "very positive," and at a deeper level is screaming with anger, fear, and a feeling of hopelessness he or she will never admit—a program for death.

I know I was also much more accepting of things as they

were. I didn't feel that the radiation *had* to work; but I was more open to whatever would happen. At the meditation retreat, the one I undertook immediately before starting radiation, I finally understood what Jack Kornfield was saying about being totally open to each moment as it came, being totally accepting and unjudging of it.

I believe the most wonderful example of the health-giving power of acceptance I have ever encountered is embodied in Brother Dodsman, whom I met at a monastery near Vancouver. He has advanced lymphoma and should have died years ago. He is unbelievably accepting of his condition and says things like, "Bring on the pain—I would love to die tomorrow because I would see God." Because his faith is so strong and he absolutely believes he is telling the truth, he keeps on living. I think because he is so accepting of his condition, there is no contention in his body at all, and so he lives on.

As well as letting go of the idea that radiation had to work, I had finally let go of needing Doris in order to live. I was still angry and bitter and the two of us had many clashes to come, but sometime during the summer before radiation, I accepted that I could live my life without her. I believe all of this allowed the radiation to work and I am convinced it would not have worked otherwise.

This past autumn a cancer patient called me for help. He had a brain tumor, and his doctor had advised radiation. It was hard to do over the phone, but I tried to persuade him to give himself some time to get ready, to work on some visualizations, at least, and to consider other possibilities as well. I found out the next week that he had already started his treatment—he just went ahead. It will be interesting to see how it works out for him.

Radiation is unlike chemotherapy and surgery, which doctors seem to be able to do to you endlessly. Rarely can you be given a course of radiation more than once. It seems to me that if you're fighting for life and health, it's not only wise but absolutely essential that you create the optimum conditions before you start that treatment.

On Cancer Patients
and Conventional Medicine

I had time in 1984 to reflect on how much my beliefs about doctors and medical treatment have changed in the past eight years, and they have changed considerably since my days as hospital administrator, when I was part of the system. I have learned a lot and I still wonder about a lot of things.

I wonder, for example, what would have happened if I had kept my basic conventional attitude that doctors "know best." Even after I had been misdiagnosed *twice* in three months, I went back to the same doctor for more of his "good medicine." Only at my insistence did he order a CAT scan, which led to the cancer diagnosis. And he did it to humor me. I know that until then, until pushed by my own intuition and frustration, I preferred to believe the doctors knew it all. It had been reassuring to know I was "in good hands," and as long as the doctor took the responsibility of figuring it out and fixing it, I didn't have to take any responsibility myself. This made it easy for both of us but I'm sure now that it would not have made me well.

Also, when I acted as though the doctor knew everything, and I knew nothing, it made it easy for the doctor to act as though his apparent total knowledge and my apparent ignorance were actual. This didn't improve my health but it was easy. We both colluded in perpetuating that myth until I became curious (significantly, I find the word "curious" comes from a Latin root word that means "cure"), until I began to find out some information myself, to make some decisions on that information although sometimes my doctors didn't agree with me. I began to see that while doctors do know some things, there is much they don't know, especially about cancer. I wish I knew more of them who would admit it more often. I began to see that there are some things about my own body that I know better than anyone else can ever know. Tapping and using that knowledge, and putting it together with what the doctors know, were important in my moving toward recovery and good health.

In spite of my own experiences of misdiagnosis, I am still surprised by the number of misdiagnosis stories I hear from people I work with in Hope. It's not that mistakes are made, but the *certainty* with which they are made that makes me wonder. I wonder about the length of time it takes to get a diagnosis—often because of the certainty with which common cancer symptoms (chronic fatigue, backache, depression, a sore that won't heal) are dismissed. A friend tells me of having two small basal cell carcinomas removed from her face recently by a dermatologist. She had to *demand* a referral when her own doctor dismissed the spots as just "two of those barnacles of life you can expect at your age."

The certainty with which the doctors say, "I got it all" also makes me wonder. Most of the members in our cancer support groups are coping with recurrences after the doctors "got it all." Their belief that the doctors were right— they were so certain—lulled them into a false sense of security that kept them from starting a get-well and stay-well program to build up their immune systems, their bodies, and their minds against the possibility of recurrence. Since there is a 60 to 80 percent chance of recurrence (very high, no matter whose figures you use), I wonder why doctors don't help us prepare for the possibility. I also wonder why some doctors who have nothing in their repertoire of treatment will say, again with certainty, "Your cancer is untreatable," leaving the patient with no hope— hardly an emotionally healthy state. One of the more aware, Dr. Irving Oyle, writes in *The New American Medicine Show,* "I know a specialist who feels the thing that is killing his cancer patients is the belief they have an incurable disease." My doctors' certainty that my tumor was untreatable and the ringing slogan "Cancer kills" kept me from challenging that verdict for almost two years.

I wonder why there are so many things they won't tell us: the chances, the exact test results, the overall statistics? Even though in Canada we have the right to have access to our own medical records, it is difficult if not impossible to get them. No one ever says "no"—there just seems to be a process that guarantees you'll give up trying. Many cancer patients are too exhausted to keep trying, which partly has to do with the cancer personality (passive and unlikely to ask) and partly has to do with the risk you take by antagonizing the people who are treating you.

Once when a technician was busy with another patient, I picked up my chart and started reading it. When the technician came back in the room and saw what I was doing, she exploded and scolded me as though I were a schoolboy. Since she was the technician who administered the intravenous needle before the scan, I didn't feel good about her being angry with me. It's not to your advantage to risk angering those who treat you and, in more crucial situations, literally have your life in their hands.

With some doctors there was either no information, or else opinion announced as certainty. I longed for that comfortable human ground in between where we could compare observations, speculate, and discuss possibilities. I had to know as much as possible because I believe that those who want to take control over their own health and lives must know the facts. I believe that fear of the unknown ("If everything is going well, why am I on painkillers and why am I still in the hospital?") is much worse than the fear of the known. You have a chance to overcome the fear that you know.

Mark, a member of the Hope group who had testicular cancer, was told he had six months to live. I attended his funeral six months and ten days later. Did the doctor program Mark to die? Would he have lived longer if he hadn't known? No one knows, but what I do know is that Mark did have the time to prepare for his death, and he did have a chance to try an alternative treatment, which, while it did not keep him alive, gave him hope and direction while he lived. I visited him right to the end and saw that his attitude was positive because he was doing something for himself, and as a result his pain was minimal.

Susan Sontag in her book *Illness as Metaphor* says, "In France and Italy it is still the rule for doctors to communicate a cancer diagnosis to the patient's family but not to the patient; doctors consider that the truth will be intolerable to all but the exceptionally mature and intelligent patient." I believe this paternalistic attitude exists to some extent in North America—and there is some support for it. Sometimes the patient doesn't want to know. Dr. Basil Stoll of St. Thomas' Hospital in London, in *Mind and Cancer Prognosis,* cites a 1976 study: "Macintosh found that of 74 patients who had a diagnosed but undisclosed malignancy, 88% knew or suspected that they had cancer. Of these patients, the majority did not want definite confirmation." To me this is an amazing statement of the willingness of the cancer patient to stay in denial and give over control. Stoll concludes, "Given this finding, it is necessary for more investigation to be conducted of patient's wishes regarding the disclosure of information about prognosis and other aspects of the disease." I believe you *have* to know to begin to get well.

Another thing I wonder about is why we allow ourselves to be treated as though we have no rights. I think sometimes it's partly the low self-esteem in which cancer patients typically hold themselves, and partly it's the fatigue. Until I finally exploded in the waiting room of the Cancer Clinic, I waited two to three hours for appointments. Other patients tell me this is the rule for them rather than the exception.

My image of the Cancer Clinic waiting room is of forty or fifty people sitting, a few talking but most of them silent, looking old and tired, waiting for their names to be called. I noted in my journal one day, "I can't tell if they are frightened, have given up, or are just glad to be sitting down on this hot day." It seemed we were sheep perpetuating a system that gives twenty people nine o'clock appointments and twenty people noon appointments and then lets everyone await the convenience of the staff. It totally confirms our feelings of low self-worth: we know where we stand on the priority list here. It builds up the anger and resentment the typical cancer patient feels but will not express.

Maybe we deserve what we get. I only knew that I didn't want it and wouldn't stand for it and I let my anger out. I revolted, but unfortunately the sheep didn't follow. They only watched, and my subsequent short waits were at their expense.

I wonder why many doctors simply decide on the treatment and then announce it to the patient along with the date and time (of the biopsy, surgery, radiation, chemotherapy), totally bypassing the consultative process. The message is "Be there!" I wonder why the patients, who have competently managed at least some of life's decisions—choosing a mate, buying a house or a car, negotiating a loan—choose this time to "play dead"—figuratively, and unfortunately for many, literally. Often the doctor-patient conversation ends with the patient not knowing the type of cancer, the prognosis, the duration, or the nature of the treatment. These are not paranoid ravings, but stories told and confirmed over and over again.

A study done by Dr. F. Holden in 1978 indicates that cancer patients who participated in their own treatment did *substantially* better than those who were passive recipients.

I wonder why more doctors don't increase their chances and the patient's chances of success by involving them in the treatment, starting at the decision-making level. I wonder why more patients don't demand it. Perhaps we are all victims of the same historical factor that kept people from accepting Jenner's concept of inoculating against smallpox (until the microscope was invented and they could see the germs); from accepting pasteurization of milk (this took twenty years); and from accepting the Pap smear test (twenty-five years). Even in the face of evidence, we just can't easily believe.

Also I think it's interesting that in the doctor-only decisions for treatment, the patient has a good chance of predicting beforehand what treatment will be offered. Dr. Lucien Israel, in his book *Conquering Cancer,* observes that if your cancer specialist is a surgeon, chances are you'll have surgery; if a radiologist, you'll have radiation; and if your specialist is a medical oncologist, chances are you'll have chemotherapy. His concept seems like something worth thinking about.

I wonder why doctors aren't more open to other methods of treatment as well as the conventional radiation, chemotherapy, and surgery. My guess is that the conventional medical model of attacking the disease—sometimes at the expense of the healthy part around it—is more deeply entrenched than we can imagine. Most cancer specialists view the holistic alternatives, most of which focus on supporting body wellness, as being foreign, out of range, and even off the wall. Cancer treatment is still in the Dark Ages in spite of the billions spent each year. The medical model addresses mainly the physical and yet the disease is so obviously emotional and psychosocial.

Surely the conventional and alternative treatments can complement each other, the alternative strengthening the mind and healthy body cells, the conventional attacking the disease. I became aware of the difference in the approaches in another way at the Ram Dass workshop in 1979. One day, in my journal, I compared the Death and Dying Workshop atmosphere to the hospital atmosphere that I knew so well from my work as a hospital administrator:

Workshop	*Hospital*
• Few rules, no signs, behavior comes out of concern for each other.	• Rules, roles, QUIET PLEASE signs, prescribed "ways to be."

- Serious but joyful; a sharing of problems.
- Austere but beautiful desert.
- Fruits, vegetables, and cereals all fresh and well prepared.

- Little humor, no joy, lots of political infighting.
- Sterile, crisp white, and stainless steel.
- Canned fruit, overcooked vegetables — often lukewarm, some "junk food."

I chuckle at Norman Cousins's comment in *Anatomy of an Illness:* "I had a fast-growing conviction that a hospital is no place for a person who is seriously ill." And I agree.

It would have been so much easier if I had not had to discover so many things on my own. I wonder when doctors will begin routinely and specifically to prescribe the obvious—sound nutrition, regular exercise, and support groups—and insist that the cancer patient learn and practice at least one of the silent healers—meditation, visualization, or other relaxation techniques.

I wonder when all cancer specialists will start examining the causes (emotions and beliefs) instead of merely treating the symptoms (the wild cells in the body).

I wonder what would happen if they did. My guess is that the rate of recurrence would drop dramatically.

And I wonder when cancer patients will realize that they must become active partners with aware doctors if they are to get well and stay well.

On Relationships

I can finally accept after sixteen years of marriage, raising four children, and sharing a variety of life-styles that I will always have some connection with Doris. Today our relationship is easy, I can be with her or not be with her, and the emotional upsets are over. I do love her and probably always will. However, in retrospect I see how terrible and typical the connection was between the trauma of our separation and my cancer.

In *Getting Well Again,* early medical records are cited to demonstrate the tie between illness and the loss of a loved one:

Gendron, 1701: "Mrs. Emerson, upon the death of their daughter underwent great affliction and perceived her breast to swell, which soon after grew painful. At last it broke out in a most inveterate cancer, which consumed a great part of it in a short time. She had always enjoyed a perfect state of health."

Nunn, 1822, noted the case of a woman whose illness started "with a shock to her nervous system caused by the death of her husband. Shortly thereafter the tumor again increased in size and the patient died."

The illness-relationship connection was also discussed in other books I was reading. For example:

An emotional need and a significant event together determine the time of illness (Arnold A. Hutschnecker).

The birth or death of a love may determine the victory of the will to live or the wish to die (Hutschnecker).

Clearly, the loss of a crucial relationship, which had occurred in the lives of 72% of the [cancer] patients, was the most significant clue in my search for possible relationships between the life history of the individual and a vulnerability to cancer (Dr. Lawrence LeShan).

The biggest single factor that I can find as a predisposing factor to the actual development of the disease [cancer], is the loss of a serious love object, occurring six months to eighteen months prior to the diagnosis (noted in my journal during a presentation by Stephanie Matthews-Simonton).

After intensive work with over a hundred cancer patients in the Hope program, I should be able to write almost a hundred case histories myself, all variations on the same theme of relationships that aren't working. But often the difficulty in a relationship is more obvious to those of us looking on than it is to the cancer patient. We see a demanding husband, a wife who won't hear, a couple who don't talk—don't *really* talk—about what's happening. Obvious to the outsider, it is unseen or deliberately ignored by the cancer patient.

If I could say only *one* thing to those who come to the program it would be, Look at your relationships—with your partner, your children, your parents, or your job. *Really* look. If you don't get your important relationships in order, the rest of your efforts will simply maintain you at best, and will be a waste of time at worst. Facing and sorting out your most important relationship is the catalyst that makes all the rest work.

On Purpose in Life

From 1975 to 1977, between the onset of my symptoms and the diagnosis of my tumor, I felt unwanted, unneeded, unchallenged. Between bouts of depression and self-pity, my curiosity about my symptoms and my determination to satisfy my curiosity kept me going, but it just barely sustained me and it did nothing to enhance the quality of my life. Finally, when my tumor was diagnosed in 1977, while I was still feeling unwanted and unneeded, at least I was challenged by the idea that I would beat the odds.

Perhaps the strongest single factor in whether a person

lives or dies is a goal or purpose in life. I know this is true for me and have seen it as true for others.

In 1978, six months after my first Simonton workshop, I set goals for myself and they are all goals that have kept my spirit alive, my creativity flowing, and my spiritual life vibrant. From wanting to live, I developed the will to do the things I had to do to get well. With my emotions and my mind focused on recovery, my immune system and body followed.

Kenneth Pelletier and Marcus Bach, among others, have studied the elders in cultures where people are noted for their longevity. In every one, the elders are respected for their wisdom and are needed for their physical contributions to community life. Not only do they live into their nineties and beyond, but the quality of their lives is rich because they have a purpose. Some of the older members of our Hope groups have learned the importance of establishing a purpose even late in life.

The quality of this purpose is also important because it must be for yourself, not for others. This is particularly hard for someone with cancer. People prone to cancer (cancer personalities) tend often to do things for others but not for themselves. Sometimes the distinction is a fine one, but it is an important one to make. For example, one of my goals was to write a book and two of my three reasons were selfish: one, to sort out my experiences to make sense of them (for me); two, to tell my children about my inner struggle (because *I* want them to know); and three, to help others who have cancer (and maybe this is for me too, to help me feel the struggle was for something larger than my own life). So while the product, this book, will ultimately benefit others, my purposes were mainly for myself.

Once you want something, your will follows. When your purpose is defined, you've taken the most important step: you *want* to live to achieve it. That big first step is emotional, but it gives you the spark you need to move to the next step, which is mental. I developed the will and the discipline to eat and exercise properly, to meditate and visualize, and to keep track of my wildly fluctuating emotional states. When my will lagged, when I was sick and tired and depressed, I usually got sicker. What I soon discovered was that I could not get on with what I wanted to do when I was sick. I couldn't write, for example, so I couldn't pursue my goal. So the motivator of my will was my emotion—the wanting to achieve my goal.

Both the wanting and the willing work together on another level. They stimulate the body's immune system, which, of course, works against the cancer.

The will to live, the purpose in life, can't be confused with not wanting to die, which is a passive state that often comes from a fear of dying. Fear is an emotion that generates little energy to change the situation. In fear you hold on to life, but when you have no purpose, your grasp is tenuous.

In working with cancer patients it is my fellow counsellor, Moyra White, who poses the question, "Are you afraid of dying or do you have a purpose in living?" From her own experience she knows her initial survival came from her terror of dying, but the quality of her life improved and her depression lifted only after she found a purpose in living.

However, when you do fear death, as many do, it is important to look at it. When you examine the object of your fear—death—you open up several possibilities. You can discover some beliefs that you have about death, and also some beliefs about life. Often you discover a spiritual side to yourself that could be rich. Confronting these aspects of life and death stimulated me to discover a purpose in living. Another possibility is to see that you really want to die. Recognizing it gives you the opportunity to focus on what you need to do to prepare yourself for that. While your life might not be extended, certainly the quality will improve, because even preparing for death is a goal.

For everyone, defining a purpose is all-important. As Nietzsche wrote, "He who has a *why* to live for can bear almost any *how*."

Suggested Reading

Frankl, *Man's Search for Meaning*
Hutschnecker, *The Will to Live*
Israel, *Conquering Cancer*
LeShan, *The Mechanic and the Gardener*
Pelletier, *Holistic Medicine*

One of these days the cancer research people who have had such enormous financial support and who have worked so frantically and intensively on the problem for the past thirty years will face up to the fact that psychology has an influence on tissue cells.

Karl Menninger

8

Putting My Life Together

$\textsc{After completing the}$ course of radiation, I was full of energy and optimism. I felt that this was the second time I was getting well (the first time, in the spring of 1978, had not been nearly so definite or dramatic), and I was determined not to blow it. The doctors didn't suggest it, but I asked for a referral to G. F. Strong Rehabilitation Hospital and for months went regularly for occupational and physical therapy. The day-to-day progress encouraged me. I wasn't sure how much movement I'd regain on my right side, but it was wonderful to feel my body coming back to life.

Week after week I experienced what I can only call miracles. My right leg was no longer coming down with a jolt, and I could do up my shirt buttons, tie my shoelaces, and wear my contact lenses again (I had been unable to get them in and out with only one hand). I could take a short walk in the fresh air without feeling totally exhausted, and when I took my time, I no longer stumbled. The burning pain under my right shoulder blade was disappearing and I was starting to write with my right hand again.

At first, there were some very awkward comic moments. As life came back to my right side, my arm or leg would sometimes twitch and jerk on its own. At first I found this frightening and also embarrassing, particularly if someone else was around. If I became angry, my right hand would tighten up and my arm would spasm violently as if I wanted to shake my fist. This happened a couple of times with store clerks, who must have thought I was a madman. It was a dramatic illustration of the connection between my emotions and my body. When I was well, like most people I could control my body so that when strong emotions came

up, my body was still and the other person had no hint of the
rage behind the polite smile. Now I saw that my body was
being true to my emotions and it was difficult to hide this. I
found it fascinating to have this instant direct feedback on
how my emotional energy was working.

LeShan sees people with cancer as having more emotional energy than they have ways of expressing it. He
writes, "I often found myself speculating whether cancer
might not be a selective disease that is more likely to appear
in those with the highest level of emotional force, especially
if their lives did not allow for the full venting of that force."
That made sense to me.

Hope

From the fall of 1980 to the spring of 1981 I was occupied
with attending to my diet and exercise programs, physiotherapy, and visualizations and with celebrating the
gradual reawakening of the right side of my body. As I had
more energy, I spent more of it organizing and expanding
Hope, a self-help cancer support group that I had started
out of my own need at one of my lowest points in July 1980.
One of the things Carl Simonton had emphasized in the June
1980 seminar was that cancer patients need a support
system, one made up of people other than family members. I
had so often longed to share my experiences and compare
notes and I needed more than my casual contacts in clinic
waiting rooms. When I discovered to my surprise that there
was no such group in Vancouver, I decided to start my own.

With more difficulty than I had expected I eventually
contacted a few like-minded cancer patients. We began with
a small group of six, meeting informally at my house. The
head of the B. C. Cancer Control Agency would not support
a group whose aim was to encourage people to take responsibility for their own illness and health, believing the

patients would feel guilty if they died. (Moyra's response to that is, "Doctor, if I die, I won't be worried about feeling guilty.") However, in 1980, Laurian Hetanen, a nurse at the Cancer Clinic who had taken the Simonton Therapist Training Program, helped spread the word and was invaluable in starting and helping that first year.

Since then, over 150 people have taken part and the program has grown to include regular weekend workshops, ongoing support groups, and counseling services. Over 2,000 people a year call for information and we are now compiling a workbook for those who do not have access to a group, and a manual for those who would like to start their own group. Hope is the only program of its kind in Canada. Its work and growth have become my full-time occupation and preoccupation, fulfilling two of the goals I set for myself in 1977. In the fall and winter of 1980, however, it was still a small but intensely focused group.

Panic

I felt my physical progress from December to March 1981 was slowing down, and writing was a particular source of frustration. I resisted retraining my right hand because it was excruciatingly slow. I finally compromised by writing one page with my left and then one with my right, and I started to write the book I had set as a goal in 1977. My naive fantasy then had been that I'd write a book about how I cured my brain tumor by visualizing. Simple.

Then in February and March I had a recurrence of symptoms. Everyone in the Hope group had had a recurrence at some time, except me. In fact—and unfortunately—most people came to Hope as a last-ditch effort because they'd already tried everything the doctors had to offer and it hadn't worked. By then it was hard for them to reverse the ravages of both the disease and the treatments. I had been worrying that I couldn't relate to them or offer enough because I had not had a recurrence myself, so I appeared to be solving the problem by having one.

I think two things precipitated it: First, I kept holding the thought of recurrence in my mind. I think at some level I wanted and needed to understand what it was like. Second, becoming a well person again had created an incredibly stressful situation. When I was sick, I wasn't really expected to do anything; being well demanded that I do something, make money, and be successful. Being successful meant, for me, expanding the Hope program, writing the book, and making money. I was putting a lot of pressure on myself.

When my symptoms started to recur, I panicked. I found out what it was like to have a recurrence. I began stumbling again and losing my balance, and my right arm became so bad that I could hardly write at all for a while. My leg was dragging and it weighed a ton. I started to feel that maybe my recovery *was* accidental and what I had been doing had no real value.

But I started paying closer attention to my visualization and relaxation again, and to diet and exercise. In March I went to Portland to hear Carl Simonton and as usual he reaffirmed what I was doing.

I also discovered that his beliefs were growing and changing. One of them, that the cancer patient must set goals in life, he had modified. He now felt that everyone has a purpose in life, a mission, and that for cancer patients to become well and stay well they must *discover* this purpose. I connected with that concept immediately because, of all the goals I had set for myself in 1977, two had actually taken on the urgency of missions. These were the goals of establishing a self-help group—Hope—and of writing a book about my experiences. It seemed they were both necessary to give some meaning to the past five years of my life.

Getting the Message

In my journal, I quoted Simonton as also saying, "My belief is, if I get the message from the disease, the disease will leave." The message I was supposed to get had to do with my relationship with Doris. I had known this for a long time but I was still struggling with it. From my journal late in 1980: "Fight with Doris, which started as a result of my feeling rejected, ignored, and unimportant." I had a lot of attention from her during my radiation treatments, then none once they stopped.

"Nothing can destroy my health so fast as this turmoil that starts in my body as a result of this relationship. Doris's relationship with me poisons my body in the most destructive way. Then she tells me, with the delight of Satan, that it's my responsibility and withdraws to the security of her self-righteousness. The bitch. I hate her and, yes, I want to get even with her. Can anyone who has been tortured so long by someone just turn the other cheek and not get back again? And then forgive? I don't want to forgive, I hate her. I hate her, I hate her, I hate her. . . ."

On the next day I note, "The burning pain in my right arm is back."

Another journal entry: "If Doris did to me physically what she does to me mentally, she'd be guilty of manslaughter." A few days later: "Today I have lost my car keys, have put them down in a store, lost my umbrella. I just about stepped in front of a car." Then: "Arm feels heavy, leg is weak, I'm stumbling and losing my balance, my back doesn't want to hold me up. Even my meditation and relaxation don't work when I'm in this kind of turmoil. My head just keeps going on and on and on." Jogging or anything else that exerted me to the point where I was gasping was about the only thing that helped.

Finally in September 1981, Doris said she would not see me anymore, even as a friend. We would have no relationship, period. And we didn't see each other for about a year. I learned I could live without her.

Dr. Robert Cantor in *And a Time to Live* writes, "The last and most subtle part of mourning is the final letting go of a secret hope, the wish that the loss had never occurred." When I stopped wishing that I had never lost my relationship, I started to see the tremendous benefits of the whole process, things that would never have happened if events had been different, if Doris hadn't left, if I hadn't got cancer. I began to see my resulting cancer as an opportunity. I made a list of the things that I would have missed without cancer.

I would never have:

• discovered the things I discovered about myself.
• found out what I *really* wanted to do in life.
• experienced love in such a profound way.
• been nearly as good a father to my children.
• written poetry, explored nature, written a book.

I would never have learned:

• to acknowledge my needs and ask for what I wanted.
• to want to live a life that means something to others.
• that to know myself is the best insurance program for good health.
• that to trust my own judgment is better than turning myself over to the experts.
• to recognize illness as a manifestation of my unresolved problems.

And I saw that on a more metaphysical level, the cancer gave me an opportunity to transform my life. I think it gives every cancer patient that chance if he chooses to move beyond the physical level. You seldom die quickly with cancer—it's not like a heart attack—so you have time to prepare yourself for death. It took me about three months, but I brought myself out of my recurrence, and by fall and winter I was better, reading a lot, and writing again.

Devastating Doubts

Nineteen eighty-one was a very unsettling year. Of the seven members from the first Hope group in 1980, five had died. Most were coming to Hope in the very final stages of their illness, so people died. I was afraid that Hope wasn't working, that I was fooling myself, that I was fooling them, and that I was wasting our time. Every time someone died, I went through this agony of doubt. Finally I decided that in the Hope groups I should also focus on improving the quality of life as well as on prolonging it. Over the years we have had wonderful feedback from people, relatives, and friends, who have assured us it is a worthwhile goal and that we are succeeding.

I filled my journal with quotes from the books I was reading and in February 1982 I noted, "This journal is all about cancer."

Then, between February and April, I had my real scare.

Every time something happened to someone in the group, I had doubts again. Was I right in doing it? Was I doing it right? Someone in the group would call me, sometimes in tears. There was bad news from the doctor; the primary cancer was spreading. We would talk for an hour. When we hung up, my shoulder and arm would be sore. I was starting to take it all on, and every time I was flooded with doubt.

I was having my second recurrence of symptoms.

Stumbling, off balance, and in some pain, I went to Hawaii for three weeks in February, with Flo-May, a woman I had

started to see. Simonton had six principles that he advised
all cancer patients to follow if they wanted to get well. I
could always remember five, and the sixth, which I always
forgot, was about the necessity to play and have fun. Flo-
May and I went to Hawaii to have fun.

That my doubt and my ambivalence were undermining me
was underlined by a dream I recorded on May 4. In my
dream I was walking a tightrope, holding a balancing pole
across the front of my body. On the left end of the pole was
the word "Faith" and on the right end, the word "Doubt."
The Doubt end kept pulling down, pulling me over. I
struggled with it, knowing as long as I let Doubt weigh me
down I would never be able to keep my balance. About a
week later my symptoms started clearing up. Somehow my
body got the message. If this sounds unbelievable, here's
the explanation that I received in December 1983. I had a
dream in which I said to myself, "My mind is bugged." When
I woke up I realized what the message was: Everything that
I say to myself (asleep or awake, it seems) can be heard by
my body.

Again, it took about three months to get over my recurrence. This time I resolved to be more consistent in all my
practices, and that was my last recurrence.

On May 24, the anniversary of Doris's leaving, I wrote, "I
must have done one hundred workshops, seminars, and
groups to explore myself and the meanings and beliefs of my
relationship with Doris. The loneliness comes up every May
24th and my arm aches." (The literature refers to the regular
recurrence of this imbedded traumatic pain as "anniversary
pain.")

In my journal of 1982 I reflected on how I had unknowing-
ly cured myself of an ulcer fifteen years before. I had a
director who called meetings frequently, ostensibly to get
our opinions, but mostly to give us his own. As we sat and
listened to his monologues, I would hold my hands over my
stomach, which always started to ache. I recall repeating to
myself over and over, "This isn't worth getting an ulcer

for"—and this cured it. I believe cancer patients who seem to be cured with no trouble must automatically and unconsciously be doing something like this. Without being aware of it, I had experienced the truth of a statement I had noted in my February journal, that a *held* thought is a powerful thought.

Putting Money in Perspective

In 1982 I was starting to focus on my relationship toward money. I had had all four of the children with me for some time now and I was pleased to be making a home for them. Because with Bub and Del I had done major and creative renovations to our own house, people asked me to do minor renovations and build decks for them, so I earned money that way. But I wanted to spend more time with Hope, being there for the people, keeping up to date by reading and going to seminars, and promoting and advertising the program. I soon realized I couldn't do carpentry *and* work with Hope. I decided that if I did what I wanted to do, that is, got on with my mission, the money would take care of itself.

In five years of making myself well again I had spent all the money I had saved, and even sold my share in the Cortes property, which was really hard. That was like selling a dream. Almost as hard had been asking my parents for money, but they proved to be both gracious and generous. I had also borrowed from Bub and Del, and at one time I owed Del over $3,000. I always told myself that I would borrow against the house, or even sell it if I had to. I told myself that when I got well I could always make money. It has not been that easy, but at this writing, I am well and out of debt.

I can never understand people with cancer who won't do things to make themselves well and who use money as the excuse. Some use their diminishing energy to stay on the job until the last possible moment (and we talk about them as though they're heroes). They then spend some time at home and in the hospital, then die and leave the family a pension. They must think that in weighing the two, the family would rather have the money than have them. We had a woman in the Hope group who lived in a middle-to-upper-class area and was financially secure, but she couldn't bring herself to go to seminars or workshops that might have been of tremendous help to her "because they cost too much"—$50 to $100. I guess she really didn't want to live.

One man in the Hope group was going to inherit some money—but he needed it now, not later. He repeatedly resisted the group's urgings to ask for some of it right away and he seemed to be saying, "I'd rather die than ask my father for money." (However, he finally did ask, took time out from work to pursue his interests, and is doing well today.)

When I truly believed that I would have the money I needed to get well, no matter what, the money came. When I wanted and needed Doris to accompany me to the Philippines, money was a real problem for her. Two friends, without being asked, gave her $1,000.

Perhaps the best example of how this attitude works is Moyra White's story. She is, with me, one of the two surviving members of the first Hope group.

Moyra was diagnosed as having Stage 4 malignant melanoma, and in 1980 she sold everything she owned to go to the Lucas Clinic in Switzerland. The week before she left, she had only enough money to pay for a one-way ticket and for part of the treatment, but she was going. She ran a classified ad to find someone to adopt her two cats while she was away. The ad was spotted by Denny Boyd, a columnist for the *Vancouver Sun,* who got Moyra's story and put it in his column. A woman Moyra refers to as the Wonderful Cat Lady read the story and gave her $1,000.

So 1982 was about money and about learning. I spent time

reading about psychoneural immunology. I attended workshops and lectures given by Jean Houston, Richard Bandler,
Carl Simonton and Stephanie Matthews-Simonton, Buck-
minster Fuller, and Linus Pauling.

Men are not worried by things but by their ideas about things. When we meet with difficulties, become anxious or troubled, let us not blame others, but rather ourselves, that is, our ideas about things.

Epictetus

9
Stress and the Cancer Profile

M<small>Y WIFE LEFT ME, MY CHIL-</small>dren went with her, I quit my job, and my house burned down. That's stress.

I was constantly tired, depressed, and suicidal, and developed a malignant brain tumor. Those are stress symptoms.

Dr. Barbara Brown, author of *Between Health and Illness,* sums it up this way: "The harm of stress occurs when there is simply too much of it—stress for too long or too many different stresses coming too close together."

Dr. Brown's is one of many excellent books that describe stress and stress management well. Everyone living in North America should read one and act on the knowledge, particularly if you have cancer, have had cancer, or recognize yourself as being a typical cancer personality. I'm not going to talk here about the aspects of stress that are better described in the books, but rather try to relate what I know about stress to cancer growth and cancer regression. But first, here are a few facts about stress that I think are useful to keep in mind.

1. *Stress can provide the spice of life,* and death is the ultimate stress-free state. Every day is filled with hassles and crises and joyful, happy times. Good and bad, all of it can be stressful. Our objective is not necessarily to get rid of stress.
2. *It isn't the stress that wears you down; it's your response to it.* Stress management doesn't have as much to do with changing the stressful events as it has to do with changing the way you respond to them. As Dr. Irving Oyle writes in *The New American Medicine Show,* "Go-

ings-on in the social environment can't make us sick.
Worrying about them does." Dr. Brown says this in
another way: "Stress is 90% how the mind looks at
difficulties in life."

3. *The body has the same physiological reaction to both kinds
    of stress,* whether it's stress arising from good occa-
    sions—a party, a holiday, a raise—or from the negative
    events we more commonly think of as stressful. This is
    what the stress response is like: Breathing becomes
    rapid and shallow, heart rate increases, blood moves
    from the extremities to the inner parts of the body, and
    adrenaline and other hormones are released in the
    system. Your body goes on "red alert," what Hans Selye
    labels the flight-or-fight response.

4. *Unless discharged, stress accumulates over days, weeks,
    and years.* Unless you turn off the "red alert" (and our
    early predecessors could do this by fighting or running
    away), the body remains in that state and the stress
    accumulates over time.

5. *Accumulated stress makes you sick.* "This prolonged
    unabated stress from which the individual has no
    respite is primarily responsible for the development of
    stress-related disorders," says Dr. Kenneth Pelletier in
    Mind as Healer, Mind as Slayer. He states, "Most modern
    medical textbooks attribute anywhere from 50–80% of
    all disease to psychosomatic or stress-related origins."
    He is speaking of diseases such as peptic ulcer, colitis,
    bronchial asthma, atopic dermatitis, edema, hayfever,
    migraine, arthritis, amenorrhea, enuresis, impotence,
    general sexual dysfunctions, and insomnia, to name
    some. These are the illnesses, but there are other
    preillness symptoms, which Selye, the pioneer in stress
    research, has listed as predisease signs of stress. Some
    of them are general irritability; dry mouth and throat;
    impulsiveness; overwhelming urge to run, cry, or hide;
    inability to concentrate; easy fatigue; keyed-up feeling;

nervous tics; nervous laugh; grinding teeth; sweating; nightmares; restlessness; excessive appetite or loss of appetite; and increased use of cigarettes, alcohol, drugs, or tranquilizers.

6. *Stress attacks the immune system.* "Illness itself may be the ultimate defense in a desperate last-ditch effort to overcome overwhelming circumstances," writes Pelletier. "Potentially one of the most negative results of excess levels of stress is the effect on the immune system."

Achterberg, Simonton, and Matthews-Simonton in *Stress, Psychological Factors and Cancer,* diagram the relationship among stress, the immunological system, and cancer growth in Figure 1.

What they are saying, and more medical researchers are beginning to agree with them, is that stress alters the balance of hormones and other substances in the body, and the effect is that the immune system is suppressed and weakened. Dr. Arnold Hutschnecker sums it up in a sentence: "Emotional stress, like physical stress, lowers resistance to disease."

They similarly diagram the psychophysiological model of cancer *regression* in Figure 2.

So, why is it then that stress caused cancer in me and causes asthma, arthritis, or heart disease in others? It seems that each of us responds to stress in a different way because of certain characteristics of personality, and we are now able to predict the kind of disease some people will be prone to. Meyer Friedman and Ray H. Rosenman in 1974 identified the qualities and behaviors their heart patients had in common, and came up with the profile of a typical candidate for heart attack. Their findings are published in the popular *Type A Behavior and Your Heart* (a good source of information on stress). Briefly, the Type A person:

Psychophysiological Model of Cancer Growth

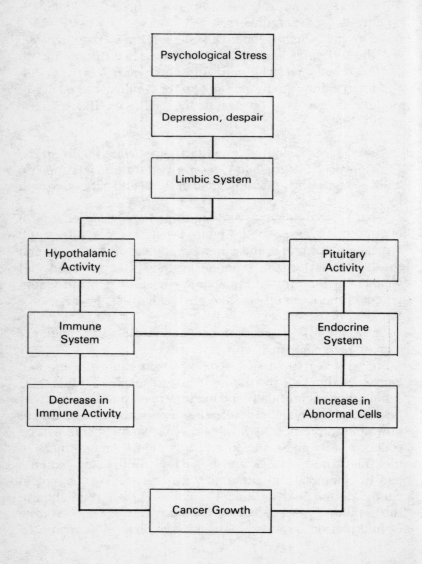

Psychophysiological Model of Cancer Regression

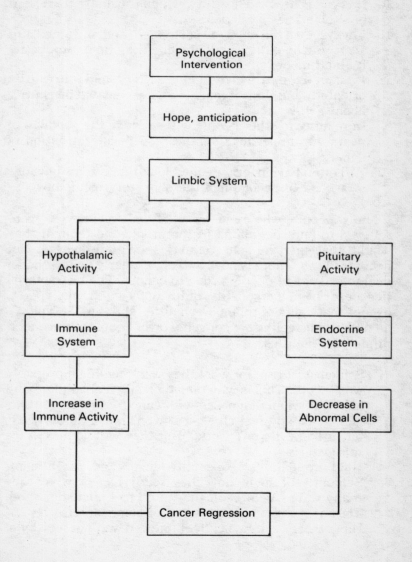

1. Has excessive competitive drive.
2. Is impatient and has a continual sense of time urgency.
3. Has easily aroused hostility, which is usually controlled but sometimes explodes.
4. Always feels the need to accomplish, and must measure accomplishments, usually by counting time, productivity, and money.
5. Is usually extroverted, aggressive, and outwardly oriented—but this often masks a deep-seated insecurity about self-worth.
6. In relating to other people will sacrifice the goodwill of peers and underlings for the respect and attention of supervisors.
7. Will often have poorly defined long-range goals because of a need to accomplish the short-term goals now.

Many people who read about Type A behavior were relieved to find they didn't fit the profile and thought they would, therefore, be safe from stress-related disease. Not necessarily so. There is now, as well, a clearly defined list of characteristics of people prone to cancer. The characteristics describe a personality quite different from Type A, except that cancer-prone personalities share with Type A's an underlying feeling of poor self-worth. People with cancer-prone personalities:

1. Seldom go all out for what they want, feeling it probably won't work. This is why they typically feel helpless and hopeless when diagnosed with cancer. As a result they lack goals and feel stuck—"It won't work unless I try, but if I try, it won't work." But they will go all out for *someone else*.
2. Hold in feelings, especially anger and resentment. Seldom talk about how they really feel or what they really want. As a result they often feel misunderstood. They will get angry on *behalf* of someone else.
3. Have a poor self-image; feel unloved and not worthy of

love, unless they are doing what others want. As a
result, they attempt to get love by being "nice."

4. Feel deeply isolated (usually from an early childhood
    life situation) but appear to be operating well. Despair
    of *ever* meeting anyone who can meet their emotional
    needs. They feel that close relationships are too risky,
    but if they finally do form a close relationship, they "put
    all their eggs in one basket," so if death or separation
    ends the relationship, they are totally devastated.

5. Have lives dominated by a problem they must solve, but
    can't. This is usually a relationship problem. They
    suffer terrible mental and emotional anguish with this
    problem and develop illness (physical pain) as a substi-
    tute for the psychic pain. It is easier for them to deal
    with physical pain than with the emotional pain.

6. Have a tendency to depression that they don't recog-
    nize.

7. Have difficulty letting go and having fun.

Achterberg, Simonton, and Matthews-Simonton in re-
viewing studies relating stress and psychological factors to
cancer point out very clear relationships. These relationships are relevant not only to the onset of cancer but to its
treatment. They summarize the findings of one study,
"Personality Characteristics as Predictors," in this way:

The idea that a loss or conflict which is perceived by
feelings of hopelessness and helplessness predates the
development of cancer by a few months was expressed
over one hundred years ago by various medical writers
and later verified by studies. Work by Blumberg and
Klopfer substantiates the hypothesis that attitudes,
emotions and personality characteristics are related to
treatment response.

After describing nineteen studies they conclude, "In
evaluating the role of stress and malignancy it appears that
any approach that would increase a person's ability to

experience more stress with fewer physical illnesses would
be a reasonable starting point."

What does all this mean to people with cancer or a
predisposition to it? What does it mean to me?

First, I have to be aware of my personal stress signals, the
things I find myself doing when I'm stressed. I eat; I sleep
more; I get speedy, frustrated, and irritable; my shoulder
and back ache; I become clumsy and unfocused; I want to
cry; I get angry; I can't concentrate; I drink coffee; I rub one
foot over the other in bed. Any one or two of these—and
sometimes I do all of them—tell me I'm stressed.

Then I have to look for the specific thing that's stressing
me. It can be a job that's not going well, anxious thoughts I
dwell on, or some interaction with a friend that I haven't
taken time to resolve. I must pinpoint the stressor.

So the initial step in stress management is becoming
aware, first that I am stressed, and second, of the specific
stressor.

Once I'm aware of the stressor, I can take the next step. I
can either change it—do something to get the job going well;
let the thoughts go; call and let my friend know how I feel
and what I want—or realize that some things can't be
changed. I can decide, for example, that my definition of the
job "going well" can be changed and I can change my
expectation, or I can turn the job over to someone else. I did
this with the hospital consulting job I took in Kelowna, after
realizing at the meditation retreat with Joseph (during my
second recurrence) that I had to give up the job or die,
which made it an easy choice. Good stress management
almost always means changing priorities. I ask myself, "Is
this worth dying for?" or conversely, "Is my life worth thirty
minutes a day for meditation, or the money it will cost to
take yoga classes, a health seminar, or some specific
training?"

Therefore, after recognizing the stress and identifying the
stressor, the second step is to change what you can change
or genuinely accept what you can't change. Psychological

stress isn't inherently in the situation or in you, but rather in the relationship between the two.

The third step is to make sure that I keep to my regular schedule of meditation and visualization and that I pay attention to diet, exercise, and support system. Meditation, visualization, progressive muscle relaxation, yoga, and other silent healers are the *only* acceptable substitutes for fight or flight (forget drugs). The silent healers can deactivate the body's "red alert" system because with any one of these practices you can control your body's autonomic system and produce physiological conditions that are the exact opposite of "red alert." Herbert Benson calls this the Relaxation Response, and its characteristics are that the respiratory and circulatory systems slow down, blood flows to the extremities from the internal organs, and the autonomic system slows down.

The third step in managing your stress, then, is to incorporate a specific practice—one of the silent healers— into your daily life, and also to take care of the *obvious:* food, exercise, and support. I've noticed that I and others in the Hope program find it hard to ask for support when we are stressed and feeling sick, but this is when we need it most. Do it.

Something else that I do when I'm stressed is take time to do something that I like—read a book, go to a movie, or listen to music. This is especially important for cancer types because they tend to take life seriously, and find it hard to play and do things for themselves.

These three steps take care of the day-to-day stresses, and will, in turn, head off long-term, built-up stress. However, for the cancer patient and cancer-prone personality, there is one additional and crucial step, and that is to find and face the dominant life problem, usually a relationship, that every cancer-prone personality seems to have. You might need the help of a counsellor or therapist. I did. But to finally sort through my relationship with Doris, which was definitely an "all my eggs in one basket" relationship, allowed the radiation to work. To finally realize that it was possible to live without her was to finally make a decision to live both emotionally and physically.

The literature is full of similar stories and conclusions drawn from them and I have quoted some in my reflections on relationships. I can repeat only what I have experienced, observed, read, and deeply believe: that to get well and stay well, the cancer patient must discover and come to terms with the life problem at the root of the cancer.

Suggested Reading

Brown, *Between Health and Illness*
Pelletier, *Mind as Healer, Mind as Slayer*
Selye, *The Stress of Life*
Simonton and Matthews-Simonton, *Getting Well Again*

Fishes and Water

Fishes, asking what water was, went to a wise fish. He told them that it was all around them, yet they still thought they were thirsty.

10

The Silent Healers

ACCORDING TO PSYCHIATRIST Steven Locke of Harvard Medical School and Boston's Beth Israel Hospital:

Teaching people relaxation techniques, self-hypnosis and biofeedback is now becoming widespread in medicine. But the idea of enhancing the immune system through relaxation, through a feeling of empowerment or by overcoming depression is one that many "hard" researchers still consider very soft indeed. And softest of all is the idea that the immune system will respond to pictures in the mind of someone who's ill. Nevertheless, research scientists are beginning to provide hard evidence that could eventually bear these theories out.

I believe it is crucial for the cancer patient to begin as soon as possible a specific stress reduction program. I call the many proven stress reduction techniques the "silent healers" because they are done in silence and they produce silence, a slowing of the body's major systems and a stilling of the autonomic nervous system. The value of techniques such as progressive muscle relaxation, self-hypnosis, auto-suggestion, autogenics, and biofeedback are discussed and described in many excellent books on stress and stress management. While I have learned and use a number of the silent healers, the two most powerful for me are meditation and visualization.

Meditation

Thoughts, and the emotions that arise from them, directly affect my body. They strengthen it when they are positive and they weaken my immune system, allowing cancer cells to grow, when they are negative, so gaining an awareness of them is crucial. If I pay attention to my thoughts, emotions, and attitudes, I can program my life.

The challenge of meditation is to examine the moment exactly as it is, accepting it just the way it is. When you focus on the moment, your mind can be like a laser, providing moments of precise insight and clarity. The concentration and focus of meditation also produce a state of relaxation when the moment is accepted exactly as it is. And to be relaxed is to promote healing. Meditation is considered by those who know about stress reduction to be the most effective of all relaxation techniques.

You may think that sitting in front of the television, meeting a friend for tea, puttering in the garden, or playing a round of golf are all effective ways of relaxing—and in one sense they are. Because you enjoy them (as opposed to other things you may have to do and don't enjoy) and they are not "work," you might think that they reduce stress. They don't necessarily. Both pleasant and unpleasant events produce stress. To relax your body and mind, you must put yourself into a state of relative stresslessness, and one of the most effective ways of doing this is to meditate.

The distinct physiological changes in your body that mark deep relaxation are also present when you are in a meditative state (slowed heart rate, respiration, and metabolism; quieted autonomic nervous system). And the other important benefit of meditation, as opposed to watching television, visiting, gardening, and golfing, is that it stills the chatter of the mind. Slowing the body's autonomic processes and stilling the mind relax your body in a most profound way and reduce the prime enemy of your immune system, stress.

So how do you do it? You focus and you practice. That's it. Easy to say and a little harder to do. You focus and you practice.

There are various forms of meditation practice—and the process is always called practice. (you *play* golf and maybe *become* a pro, but with meditation you always *practice*). You can concentrate on an external image, on an internal image, on the breath, or on mind states. Whatever you choose, you must consciously and conscientiously practice. Pelletier explains it this way:

Meditation is not a passive process but a means of allowing an individual to enter into daily activity relatively free of neurotic distractions. The main point is that the meditation relaxation is not a spontaneously occurring state that prevails in the absence of stress. Meditation and relaxation require as much diligent practice as any other skill, and must be learned and practiced in order to be effective.

Perhaps the most important shift for me was learning to observe the movement of my sensations and my thoughts, neither holding on to them because they were pleasant nor trying to get rid of them because they were unpleasant. Observing them without dwelling on them allowed them to "be" and to pass by. Observing my fears and experiencing my pain without dwelling on them or wishing them away changed the nature of fear and pain for me. And they changed not only in nature but also in duration. Trying to stop the internal dialogue about my cancer never worked, but *allowing* it to rise into my consciousness and observing it as simply another series of thoughts, in a sense freed it— and allowed it to pass away.

I soon found that I could use my ability to accept my thoughts to develop an ability to accept my cancer. To accept it and not dwell on it leaves it free, too, to change and pass away.

I learned to meditate in a retreat setting, away from the distractions of daily life, surrounded by silence and other people who were inwardly focused and intent on their practice. With brief instructions each day from the retreat master, my practice developed and deepened so that I could continue on my own when I returned home. I think this is the ideal way to learn, but I realize the ideal is not always possible. Taking instruction from someone who is an experienced meditator and meditating with that person or with a group from time to time is also a good way to get started. Reading one of the books listed at the end of this chapter will also help.

Several business friends of mine who are longtime meditators routinely attend a ten-day retreat each year, to deepen their practice, manage stress, and maintain their already abundant health and energy.

Visualization

Visualization is a powerful form of meditation because, to quote Roberto Assagioli, "images or mental pictures and ideas tend to produce the physical conditions and external acts that correspond to them." You are what you eat: you become what you see. Carl Simonton and Stephanie Matthews-Simonton were very much aware of this when they pioneered the use of visualization for self-healing of cancer patients. Their research indicated that the psychological factors of cancer can be influenced by stress reduction and visualization techniques. They found that visualization and relaxation techniques, when practiced regularly, both improved the quality of life of cancer patients and also extended it. They began their work in 1972, and although their program has grown and shifted emphasis in some ways, visualization has remained a central part of it.

In the Simonton visualization, you work from this basic "plot": Your white blood cells, your immune system, attack and destroy the cancerous material. It is a basic good-guys versus bad-guys plot and the good guys win. How you write the script around the plot is your own decision. You can be literal, seeing actual white cells attacking the shape or form your cancer has taken, in the actual part of your body where it is. Or you can write the script symbolically, as I have for myself. Once you have established the scene and the action that feels good for you—and this can take a few days—then you use that visualization three times a day. Repeating and using the same images and the same script give the process power.

While the experience is primarily visual, you can broaden it to include all the senses—taste, touch, smell, and hearing. If, right now, you close your eyes for five minutes and visualize the texture, color, shape, smell, and sound of biting a lemon, and your mouth starts to pucker when you image the taste, you're catching on. If it doesn't, more detail, concentration, and practice will help. When you can use visualization in a multisensory way like this, you can increase the impact on your thoughts, feelings, and behavior. Dr. Brugh Joy writes in *Joy's Way,* "Visualization requires exquisite control over the portion of the mind that has the power to create objects, ideas and events. . . . That it works is undeniable: How it works can only be hypothesized."

When you visualize, since your subconscious can't distinguish between a real and an imagined experience, your body responds on a muscular, glandular, cellular, and memory level just as it would if the experience were real. This belief is strongly held by professionals such as Maxwell Maltz and Roberto Assagioli, and recent research is verifying it. This research shows that both real and imagined experiences trigger the same biochemical release into the body, because the brain cannot tell the difference between the experiences. When you *think* that car running the red light is going to run into you, your body "rush" is the same as it would be if the car really *was* going to hit you. That it misses you does not undo the chemical rush or the stomach knot.

Willers

Visualization is active, programmed imagination, so it is an act of will. As such, its practice and effect depend on a strong will. Assagioli has identified seven characteristics of people he calls "Willers," and I believe effective meditators and visualizers have the characteristics of Willers.

1. Willers have the energy to create the intensity needed to overcome internal and external disruptions and distractions. The greater your energy, the greater the intensity of your focus on the image.
2. Willers have the control and discipline that are needed to regulate the process. You must be regular and consistent for visualization to be an effective, and eventually easy, process—like a good habit.
3. Concentration that comes from attention and focus is another characteristic of Willers. They are able to still the mind to focus on the image. When the image is one that is temporarily frightening or uninteresting, intention and attention help maintain concentration.
4. Willers also display determination and decisiveness.

You must be decisive about choosing the form the visualization will take and about the time and frequency of your daily practice. *Maybe* doesn't work.

5. Persistence, endurance, and patience are also qualities that Willers have. Endurance and patience are aspects of persistence. To visualize, you need to persist through early difficulties, to endure in spite of setbacks, and to be patient with yourself as you deepen your practice.

6. Willers also have initiative, and courage and daring are aspects of initiative. It takes courage to start and daring to try, particularly with something that may be new and different to you. When you begin to visualize, you must know that there are no guarantees just as there are no guarantees in life. You must have the courage to risk and to start the venture anyway.

7. Organization is the characteristic of Willers that helps them synthesize and integrate all these qualities with all parts of the practice. To practice active programmed imaging—visualization—requires all the qualities of a Willer, including this ability to put it all together. The qualities of a Willer are also the qualities we need to engage in all the practices that lead to a healthier life. Strengthening your will may not be easy, but it's possible—and necessary.

Purpose

How can you strengthen the will to make visualization more effective? First, you must have a purpose, a reason to live, and an intention to get well. You must have an intensity or passion about life. Often cancer patients have an ambivalence about living. When I experienced this ambivalence from time to time, acknowledging it helped me to accept it. (What I acknowledge I can change; what I deny I cannot.) Then I just got on with life "as if" I had an intense passion to live. Getting on "as if" can get you through the rough spots. Repeating my affirmations through my deepest physical and emotional lows "as if" I believed them kept me in touch with my deepest desire to get well, although my visible behavior seemed to be the exact opposite.

Practice

Second, you must practice to strengthen your will. The mind, like a muscle, can strengthen its qualities with practice. At the beginning, try a short visualization of about five minutes and do it six or seven times a day. Try to discover what works for you, but as in beginning any exercise, you must do it gradually.

Emotional Awareness

Third, become aware of your emotional needs and pay attention to them. Hutschnecker, in *The Will to Live,* writes, "The biological will to live seems not enough to support us through the complex stress of life in a civilized world. We need a moral and emotional force to make the struggle endurable. The will to live in civilized man is a combined biological and psychological drive." I have a notation in my journal that reads, "When I set my will in opposition to my emotions, my emotions always win." I don't know where I read that, but it is certainly true for me.

Skillful Will

Fourth, develop a skillful will, one that will help you find a strategy that works best for you, one that gives the greatest benefit for the least effort. Develop a visualization for yourself that is vivid and has something in it that excites you or speaks to you. The quality of the image is as important as the frequency of the practice. If you choose an image for your white cells, for example, make sure it isn't an army of rats if, in fact, rats frighten you or you see them as repulsive. When I saw my tumor as the rotten spot in a healthy tree, and the white blood cells as a woodpecker that routs out the rotten and diseased spot, I enjoyed the image. As a boy, I had listened to the rat-a-tat-tat of woodpeckers while lying out on the prairie grass. The image gives me pleasant memories. Because this image is consistent with the reality I want, and at the same time it produces pleasure at the image level, it sends a powerful message to my unconscious mind.

There is a growing body of "hard" data to prove that techniques such as meditation and visualization work, and there is other evidence and related research to support the hypothesis that we can effect some self-regulation of the immune system. There is strong evidence that the brain and the immune system "talk to each other" continuously, and if the mind can suppress the immune system (there is proof that depression does), then it seems reasonable to assume the mind can enhance it. As Dr. Irving Oyle puts it, "If you have mind-induced disease, why not mind-induced health?" Nicholas Hall and colleagues in the department of biochemistry at George Washington University, in a preliminary study with a small number of patients, found correlations that indicated patients improved their immunity when they practiced imaging, and lowered their state of immunity when they did not.

It was when Dr. Carl Simonton first suspected a connection between the patients' own expectations, beliefs, and images of illness and death and the progress of their cancer that he began, in 1972, to develop his present program in which visualization is central to the treatment of cancer patients. While he began then as a radiation oncologist who also used psychological techniques, he now less often chooses radiation as a treatment and relies more on techniques that actively involve the patient.

I learned to visualize at a Simonton workshop and later worked with a therapist to develop specific visualizations to use during my radiation. There are workers in the holistic health field and how-to books to help you learn to visualize. I sometimes found it hard to imagine myself in a state of vigorous health when I was feeling especially tired and depressed. It was helpful then to act "as if" I were wonderfully healthy, to picture myself "as if" I had already received the benefits of my imaging. This wasn't to deny that the fatigue and depression were happening, but to focus on the state I wanted to be in.

When you act "as if," your behavior will influence your feelings and thoughts, just as your feelings and thoughts influence your behavior. Your behavior, acting "as if" you're feeling good, will influence your thoughts—"I think I'm feeling a bit better"—which will, in turn, influence your behavior . . . and so on. Your body is a closed circuit, and visualization is one way to turn on the power.

Inner Voices

There are three other important ways to tap the inner self. They are ways of hearing your inner voice, and are most often the product of the moments when your conscious mind is silent. For example, I had the following dream:

I am in an anteroom of St. Paul's Hospital. My cousin, who I considered to be a wimp who would go along with anything, is in the operating room and I am to go in next. In the anteroom with me is my favorite aunt, and a friend, Wilma, the wife of the hospital director. I feel both these women have my welfare at heart.

Wilma suggests we go for a walk and I find myself

walking up a barren hill, at the top of which is a sacrificial altar. Wilma and Aunt Bertha stand back as I go up the ten steps to the altar. On top of the altar is a pig's head, recently butchered and running with blood. It is alive and looking at me with sad, pleading eyes. It is helpless and has no way of moving itself, and all it can do is plead with its eyes.

Now I am on the hillside again, walking down, and Wilma puts her arm around me saying, "Meditation is healing and surgery is needless."

My inner voice spoke to me in my dreams another time:

A woodpecker is effortlessly pecking in slow but regular bursts; I hear the rat-a-tat-tat sounds, and a message that is delivered in cadence with the regular tapping. "It's important to let go; let it happen; don't force it. It's important to let go; let it happen; don't force it."

Dr. Carl Jung, in *Memories, Dreams, Reflections,* speaks of working with dreams and fantasies as a way of getting in touch with the unconscious. "I avoided all theoretical points of view," he wrote, "and simply helped the patients to understand the dream-images by themselves without application to rules and theories." The ancient high priests before Jung also used dreams to heal although they surrounded the whole process with ritual. The patient journeyed to the healing shrine, underwent a period of fasting and purification, and was instructed by the priest to have a dream. On returning to the high priest, the patient was helped to interpret the dream and the two derived suggestions from it to make the patient well.

Looking at dreams is a fruitful way for all of us to explore our unconscious minds and to discover what is really happening in our lives. I have recounted here as examples two of the dozens of dreams I've recorded, to illustrate the ways in which dreams have been useful to me. From the first dream you will recognize the words "Meditation is healing and surgery is needless" as words from my unconscious mind that I later used to confirm my conscious (logical) decision not to have a craniotomy for biopsy. I identified with the image of the helpless, pleading, sacrificial animal in that dream so I knew the message was for me.

In the second dream, I heard the words as a reminder of what I had to do, and used the image as well. The woodpecker became the central image of the visualization I used hundreds of times in whittling away at my tumor. From the silence of my sleep, images and my inner voice come up again and again to guide me. I have learned to listen and to trust.

You may tell yourself that you don't dream. You do. You may tell yourself that you can't remember your dreams. You can. Like many new endeavors, it will take some practice to start recovering more of your dreams and using them. I find it helpful to address a question to my inner voice before I go to sleep, or to meditate on a situation I find puzzling. This is not to address my *conscious* mind to worry all night but to focus the unconscious movement of my dreams. In addition, I keep a pen and paper by my bed to record the words and images while they are fresh. It doesn't matter if they are fragments or don't "make sense"—I've learned to trust that they come together eventually. Jung says that your unconscious always has your best interests in mind.

You can also hear your inner voice in what I call "quiet moments." The second way of hearing messages from your unconscious is actually more direct and often easier to understand than dreams. Our inner voice speaks to us often, but we must be open to hearing it.

The day I awoke saying (out loud), "I'm going to heal myself," is an example of a message from a quiet moment, words that burst from my unconscious mind in that twilight moment between sleep and waking. For me the words often, but not always, come out in my own voice, and they always come at a time when I have been consciously struggling but seem to have little power to change the situation. Then my unconscious breaks through like the cavalry to save the day.

I believe this is what Maltz, Jung, and Assagioli are talking about when they say that the emotional imagination is much more powerful than the conscious will.

A third way to receive direction is to ask your inner guide to directly address your unconscious. The dream of myself as a tightrope walker came from a question to my inner guide. Panicked by a recurrence of symptoms, I asked my inner guide why I was stumbling and losing my balance. The spontaneous image of myself being pulled down by doubt on the one side and needing faith to maintain my balance was the answer from the inner guide.

Perhaps the power of that inner voice and inner vision, and the importance of listening and responding to it, is best shown in the story of Ollie, a Hope member, and Mike, her husband. Ollie was told by her two doctors that she would not be leaving the hospital and had, at best, two weeks to live.

She had a vivid dream that night. She was inside a black box, which she recognized as a coffin, and someone was nailing the lid shut. She struggled against the lid, finally pushing it off, and then she climbed out of the box.

The next day she called Mike to help her discharge herself from the hospital. Mike started bringing her to evening sessions with us at Hope, where she quickly became involved and worked hard. Her courage and Mike's unconditional love and support carried them through a full, virtually pain-free year. Ollie's attention to her inner voice that linked her to her fighting spirit and determination stretched her two weeks to over a year that was a treasure for her and Mike and an inspiration for the rest of us.

Suggested Reading

Benson and Klipper, *The Relaxation Response*
Bry and Bair, *Visualization*
LeShan, *How to Meditate*
Shames and Stern, *Healing with Mind Power*
Simonton and Matthews-Simonton, *Getting Well Again*

Once a man with great faith in God was caught in a flood. On the first day, when the water was up to his waist, a neighbor came by in a rowboat, calling, "Jump in and I'll take you to higher ground."

The man refused. "God will look after me," he said.

By the next day he was sitting on the roof of his house, water swirling around his feet, when another neighbor came by with a rowboat, calling, "Jump in and I'll take you to higher ground."

Again the man refused. "God will look after me," he said.

On the third day, he was standing on the roof of his house, the water lapping under his chin, when a helicopter appeared overhead. The pilot dropped a ladder, calling, "Grab on and I'll take you to dry ground."

Again the man refused. "God will look after me," he said.

On the fourth day, the man drowned and shortly he found himself at the gates of judgment, facing God.

"I don't know what happened," he said, quite bewildered. "I really believed You'd save me."

God scratched His head, equally puzzled. "I can't figure it out Myself," He said. "I know I sent two rowboats and a helicopter."

11

Talks with My Tumor

Sixteen times in my journals of 1982, I noted feeling especially creative and very good as a result. Usually it was a new "hit" about myself or about someone in the group. Being creative, I recognized, was important to my health.

By the end of the year, my spirits were high. I spent Christmas alone on Cortes Island, where I filled sixty pages in my journal with a series of unusual dialogues with my tumor. At the risk of appearing a little crazy, I'm including some excerpts here, slightly edited for easier reading. (When you talk to a tumor, you don't take time to correct grammar and insert punctuation.)

The conversations started when I was doing visualizations. The first time the tumor spoke, I opened my eyes to stop the images and the voice. I didn't want to hear it. It happened twice more and I resisted twice before I finally gave in. When I did, the words flowed out of me—it was what I have imagined channeled writing to be like.

Dec. 25—Christmas Day

T: You know I'm your friend.
ME: Well, I'm really very tired of the struggle and want to get rid of you. I feel silly talking to you—it makes me feel like I'm crazy.
T: That's one of the reasons I'm still here—you sure have a lot to learn.
ME: What do you mean?
T: For one thing, you're still caught up in what people think. You are here to serve people, not to impress them. I tried to tell you one month ago but each time you started to visualize and heard my voice you got up and stopped. I tell you again—you have a lot to learn.

It's important you learn to trust yourself and give up your doubts. I'm here to teach. Appreciate it instead of fighting it. The only way you'll get rid of me is to smarten up.

You've got a purpose in life and you've got to acknowledge it without feeling silly. You know when you feel creative and when you make a difference that you feel good. Feeling good is what health is about.

So you're feeling that ache in your right shoulder blade and the weakness in your right arm. Very familiar feeling—right? Immediately your mind thinks, I'm growing larger and will eventually do you in. Then your fear makes you feel helpless. You try to ignore it and that doesn't work and never has. You try to sleep it off and that makes you depressed. So I suggest you quit wasting time and deal with situations as they arise.

ME: Great bloody advice. Deal with what? Easy for you to say but hard to do—don't you know I don't know what to do?

T: You do know and you also know it takes work, persistence, and courage. Courage to do what you have to do and the courage to be yourself. Of course, this means you may not be the nice guy anymore. Are you afraid of people laughing at you and thinking you're nuts?

I know you've changed many things and I have helped you. I admit [laughing] I did use a little force— you experienced it as being without choice and feeling helpless. There's always a choice—it's just that you don't like some of the choices. It's mostly because there is too much fear involved, fear of something in the future. You fear because your choice will make you unhappy; it comes down to the fear of "not getting." The more you worry about not getting something or someone, the more likely it will occur. Worry is useless.

ME: Okay, tell me, how do I deal with worry?

T: Face the fear. One of your favorite authors, Paul Tillich, calls this "the courage to be." To be yourself, to be true to yourself, is to truly participate in life and this is always health-giving.

     I will just disappear one day when you no longer need me.

ME: I'd like to believe that. When?

T: That's your choice. You've told members in Hope many times, "It isn't easy—but it's possible." You slip so easily into self-doubt and self-pity. Remember when Don Juan teaches Casteneda to be a warrior. He says, "A warrior has no time for self-pity, he can't afford this indulgence." Neither can you or those others in Hope. Self-pity is a deadly trap. It leads to depression. In the gray world of depression, there are "no ways." Nothing seems possible or worthwhile. It's a form of dying. Do you see how I'm aiding you?

ME   (feeling angry): No, I don't!

T: Yes, you do—look at it. You know that depression has physiological consequences. Prolonged depression will depress your immune system, and when that doesn't function, you are open to any disease, with no resistance to fight it.

ME: Yes, I know if I let down, you may start to grow again. You're a bastaid and I hate you for putting me in this position. I'm incredibly tired—I don't want to keep on struggling. Yes, I feel sorry for myself. Why shouldn't I?

T: I never told you not to be depressed or feel sorry for yourself; that won't stop it from happening. I'm saying you have to be aware of the dire consequences. The further you dig yourself into the pit, the harder it is to climb out. The paradox is that you must allow yourself to experience depressions without getting stuck in them. This is enough for today. Forget about your cold; go out jogging or take a walk along the beach and relax.

December 26

T: Good morning.

ME: I feel so strange talking to you.

T: Forget about being so damned logical all the time. You
       feel everything has to make sense and be rational.
       This is the way you block yourself from your feelings
       and your subconscious. It makes you feel strange
       when you're doing something extraordinary like talk-
       ing to me. After all, I am just as much part of you as
       your arm or leg. Do you believe I'm real?

ME: Oh, I know you're real. I saw a picture of you on the
       CAT scan and I know it was you who paralyzed my
       right side.

T: Are you aware I saved your life? Every situation in life
       has two sides to it—like a coin. Because you see only
       one side doesn't mean that the other doesn't exist.

       You tell Hope members that cancer, like the Chi-
       nese symbol for crisis, has two parts; the top symbol
       indicates danger, the bottom one opportunity. Learn-
       ing to see both sides of every situation is to broaden
       your reality. Crisis is dark and cloudy, but always has
       a bright side. So has cancer.

ME: You saved my life?

T: What about the time when you didn't want to live?

ME: Oh, that. You mean when I contemplated suicide?

T: Strange, isn't it? You would consider taking your own
       life, and then when the doctors told you about me and
       what little chance you had, you discovered you did
       want to live. Of course, to die from cancer is far more
       acceptable than to die by suicide.

December 27—11 A.M.

T: Here I am again.

ME: I should have a name for you.

T: Never mind that. Think of me as a navigator.

ME: That's a strange way to think of you. I've always thought of you as my enemy.

T: Initially you needed to fight and not be so passive. But at this stage it is wrong thinking to see me as an enemy. When you see me as an enemy who could kill you, you are afraid. Being fearful of me keeps you from seeing things as they really are. Extreme fear even paralyzes.

ME: Yes, I do fear you. I know that even if you grow only slightly, I could get backaches, lose my balance, have my arm dangle again, and slobber when I eat. You can raise my anxiety level in no time. I start feeling trapped and helpless.

T: Do you think I threaten your existence?

ME: Of course I do, you asshole.

T: Okay, don't get mad. You're angry now—that's how you react when you feel trapped. It's a way of not acknowledging your fear. Face your fear squarely. Don't block it.

ME: I worry about becoming a cripple.

T: You have a choice. What's happening to you? Do you hear yourself? You sound like a victim—as if some external force is doing it to you and you have nothing to do with it. A victim always feels hopeless, helpless, and in despair. When you see you have something to do with creating me and start taking responsibility, these feelings lessen. Take each situation as it comes and there will be movement in your life. The crucial part is how you respond and what attitude you take.

ME: You threaten me and then give me good advice.

T: Remember Victor Frankl's book *Man's Search for Meaning*? He saw that the prisoners who were stripped of absolutely every human dignity and all human possessions and survived were the ones who retained an attitude of having choice. Their beliefs and attitudes saved their lives. Your beliefs and attitudes are absolutely crucial to your health and particularly to your cancer because of all the myths around it. Have you heard of attitudinal healing? Your attitude is vital and will determine whether you live or die and the quality of your life.

ME: I believe you. Okay, get on with telling me how you're my friend and not my enemy.

T: Hold on, I never said that. You are putting words in my mouth. I said, "I am your friend," I did not say, "I am not your enemy." I'm both your friend and your enemy. You are well aware of me as an enemy, but consider for a minute that I'm your friend. Tell the people in your group that cancer can be their friend.

ME: Yeah, sure, they'd think I was nuts and they'd be right.

T: Okay, just consider the possibility for yourself. Remember when you considered taking your own life, when I came along, I gave you something to fight for. During the two years your problem was considered psychosomatic, you felt awful and your friends weren't too sympathetic. When the doctor found me, your problem became organic and both you and your friends liked it better.

ME: It's always easier to deal with the known than the unknown.

T: You certainly learned a lot during these last seven years.

ME: Yes, far more than the previous forty, and I do appreciate this learning.

T: Good, it's about time you started acknowledging yourself. That's growth. You need self-esteem to be healthy.

ME: It's hard to feel self-esteem when my needs aren't getting met.

T: You sure do feel sorry for yourself. Everyone has

needs for love, care, understanding, and a purpose in life. When yours weren't met, I came along. It's a negative way to get attention but people do it all the time.

ME: Yes, that's true. Getting sick was a way I could deal with the tremendous emotional pain I had—anything seemed better than that. I put myself down and so did others because I couldn't handle the pain around my divorce. I no longer do this or let others do it. I did the best I could at the time.

December 28—10:30 A.M.

T: I'm here if you want to talk.

ME: Yes, I do. When I was waking up this morning, a Maxwell Maltz statement about imagined experiences came to mind. In his book he talked not only about getting what you imagine but also that an imagined experience has the same physiological effects as the real experience.

T: Yes. What is the point you're trying to make?

ME: Well, if I can imagine pleasant experiences, the neurotransmitter in my brain will, in turn, send messages to my endocrine system, and hormones that are conducive to my health will be released.

T: You're on the right track—of course you realize this is a two-way process. An imagined negative experience works in the same way and generates hormones destructive to your health. Your body cannot distinguish between "real" and imagined experiences and simply responds to the pictures in your "mind's eye."

The prolonged images have the most direct effect on your physical body. The negative images such as anger, frustration, and resentment tend to be prolonged. For example, the fear and anxiety that you experience are likely to be more prolonged than feelings of joy and harmony.

ME: Why is that?

T:　What you call negative emotions such as fear and anxiety are feeling states you don't like, so you try to push them away. You do this by denying these feelings are there. This, of course, never works. It's like pushing a large rubber ball you can't stand looking at, under the water. While you hold it under, it appears to be gone and you don't have to look at it, but as soon as you move your hand and release it, it pops back up. You can appreciate how much energy is required to constantly hold your emotions underwater. What you resist, persists. You resist looking at negative emotions rather than deal with them so they persist. Then you feel stuck, trapped, and helpless. This puts incredible stress on your body.

When you have positive emotions such as joy, your pain temporarily stops and so does the stress. Positive emotions generate the most powerful healing drugs. Your brain is more than a computer. It is a sophisticated pharmacy with all the drugs necessary to heal yourself.

ME:　Yes, but get back to why positive emotions don't last as long as negative ones.

T:　When you are in a state of joy, you are just enjoying; you aren't thinking about enjoying. But then you start thinking, "Hey, I'm enjoying myself. What can I do to stay in this state?" As soon as you hang on and try to make it last, it evaporates.

ME:　Do you mean if I'm feeling fear, I should try to hang on to it?

T:　Yes, but not exactly the way you think of it. When you allow yourself to experience the fear, to explore it, get curious about it, play with it, and look at it from all angles, you will experience a shift, and experience less fear. The only way you can understand this is to try it.

ME:　Why are you talking so much about emotion?

T: Because your emotions are what allowed me to grow. Haven't you seen that over and over again in yourself and in your work with cancer patients? Emotions are the root cause. And emotions reflect your beliefs and attitudes. You have to explore your beliefs and attitudes, especially if you want to get well and stay well.

ME: Yes, I know lots of people who are temporarily well after surgery, chemotherapy, and radiation. Most of those who come to Hope were considered well after treatment, but then they have a recurrence. The physical treatment can be useful but the emotions still have to be looked at, I can see. I've even read studies that back this up.

T: I know you know that. I hear you tell your group that cancer is a message.

ME: Yes, I get discouraged when they think the doctor's "I got it all" means "Goodbye cancer." It makes them feel so good they stop working at the stuff that triggered the cancer in the first place.

December 29

ME: You promised earlier on you'd tell about what I could do to eventually get rid of you.

T: Come on, Claude, you've read Selye and talked to him.

ME: Yes, I did.

T: Then you are aware of the bottom line. Prolonged stress eventually leads to death because stress breaks down the immune system and leaves the body vulnerable to infection. Prolonged stress attacks the weakest link in your body. Medically, this is called a predisposition to a certain disease. Your emotional makeup has more to do with this than heredity has. In fact, you have learned to be aware of your own stress, which is not an easy job. You've both reduced it and also learned to cope with it more effectively. If you had not discovered that your thoughts can be the biggest stressor, I might have done you in. As soon as you started reducing stress, the chemicals in your body contained me and then started whittling me down. Remember how I grew when you were so stressed doing that hospital planning job in Vernon?

ME: Okay, okay. What else can I do?

T: You can exercise, eat properly, have a positive mental attitude, and put yourself in an environment conducive to healing.

ME: Oh.

T: You sound disappointed. Did you expect something more esoteric?

ME: I hoped it would be powerful, unusual, and fast.

T: They are powerful, but not unusual or fast. They are called the four horsemen of health. They are so simple that you didn't even pick up on a powerful dream you once had. The obvious can be blinding. Do you remember your dream in which you were playing cards and you were dealt four aces? Four aces in the hole is a winning hand, but only if you play them.

ME: Yes, in my dream I felt confused about the rules. I didn't turn the cards up and I lost the game.

T: Yes, the cards are useless unless you play them. Trust yourself more. You have a winning hand.

ME: God, I'm dumb.

T: Claude, one of the aces is a positive attitude and it's not positive to keep telling yourself you're dumb.

December 30, 1982—noon

T: Good morning. We had agreed to continue at ten A.M.

ME: Yes, but last night I went . . .

T: Excuses. Excuses.

ME: But . . .

T: I'm not criticizing you, I just want to point out that a commitment is a commitment. It's important to health to keep it. Your health requires commitment and without it you won't get anywhere. Discipline is also important to health and you discipline yourself by keeping your commitments.

ME: I think illness is an expression of a deep struggle going on inside.

T: Where did you read that?

ME: I don't remember but it makes sense to me.

T: Yes, there is a physical struggle going on in most cancer patients, the struggle between defense cells and the malignant cells which are out of control and on a rampage. There is also an emotional struggle that has been going on for some time before the first symptom appears. Psychological studies have proved this. You weren't aware of the physical symptoms your emotional struggles could trigger. Dr. Walter Cannon in *The Wisdom of the Body* says when stress messages are ignored, they become symptoms, and then disease, until your body gets the message. Your inner struggle was accentuated by your "everything is fine" attitude. Your denial led to disease and would have led to death eventually. See, I saved your life.

December 31

ME: You know, being by myself for seven days makes me feel great. On the radio this morning, John Denver was singing, "Welcome to this morning, welcome to this day, I'm the one that made it this way. It's perfect."

T: What you're doing is very healing.

ME: What's that?

T: Giving yourself time all by yourself. It gave us time to have this talk. There were too many distractions back home.

New Year's Day, 1983

T: Healthy, Happy New Year, and welcome to 1983. Have you made any resolutions?

ME: I'm not much for resolutions, although I do want to write. Last year I seemed to be almost totally preoccupied by health; this year it will probably be writing and Hope.

T: Yes, creativity is important in healing. Jung talks about man's life being a balance between his creative and destructive aspects. When there are too many negatives, the balance is upset and the body breaks down. If you can see and feel yourself as a part of the Universal Creator, you experience a whole different level of creativity.

ME: Sometimes I feel this. I used to see God as something outside myself and I sense now that there is no division. I'm a part of God like the waves outside my door are part of the ocean. I don't want to talk about it. I like to experience God as something that's real, like my experience at Joseph's meditation retreat. I have much more faith in myself. I once heard Ram Dass say you have faith after experiencing thousands of doubts. I've had many doubts about myself.

T: This faith is not just "blind faith." There is no such thing as blind faith. Either you have faith or you don't. You can't decide to have faith, but you can "act as if" you have faith and operate from that basis until you do have faith—or don't.

ME: Say more.

T: The element of doubt is a condition of life. It can threaten your life when you are in total doubt. In your case, if you have doubts about what you can do to regain your health, you can still believe that whatever you do will be appropriate for you. This is conviction which is a state of faith and trust. You can proceed

without the guarantee and assurances you would like.
Mistakes are okay. They only signal a time to change
direction. There is no learning without trial and error.

ME: I've sure made a lot of mistakes over the years.

T: You're learning. I've diminished in size and eventually
I will be gone. It is only experience that moves. Your
most dramatic and painful experiences have moved
you forward. Experience moves you from belief into
knowing.

America's loss of faith in the medical
establishment gave a strong symbolic push
to the paradigm shift from institutional
help to self-help. When we entered the
1970's without the long promised cure for
cancer, people began to question the om-
nipotence of science.

John Naisbitt, *Megatrends*

12

Pay Attention to the Obvious

Diet and Nutrition

Vegetable—from a root word meaning "full of life."
Diet—from a root word meaning "way of living."

More than ever, there is solid evidence that not only does stress precipitate cancer but the psychological changes accompanying stress inhibit the body's immune mechanism. Other evidence suggests that good nutrition is a factor in reducing stress, and further, that a proper diet can improve the functioning of the immune system. I know of no special diet that will single-handedly cure your cancer, although some are purported to. I do know that a good diet will improve your health greatly. Some authorities now go further to say that what we eat directly affects the immune system.

In the past, there have been controversial claims made about diet but some common factors are emerging that are generally agreed on by nutrition experts. The National Academy of Sciences, in the United States, after years of study came out in 1984 with a 600-page report on nutrition. In a nutshell, the report advises people to eat less fat (suggesting a 25 percent reduction); little salt-cured, pickled, and smoked food; and more fresh vegetables, fruits, and whole grains. This diet will not cure cancer, but will reduce the risk of developing it. It urges the use of food rich in Vitamins A and C, pointing out that foods rich in Vitamin C can inhibit the formation of cancer-causing substances. In 1985, the American Cancer Society basically accepted these recommendations. Consistent with this, I put forward the following guidelines to members of the Hope group:

Intelligently reduce or eliminate:

1. Fats and oils
2. Sugar, salt, white flour
3. Red meat
4. Overly processed foods
5. Additives and preservatives
6. Alcohol, cigarettes, smoking, unnecessary prescription and nonprescription drugs, coffee, tea, chocolate, soft drinks
7. Dairy products (especially for patients with breast cancer)

While it's impossible to avoid all these substances, you are advised to reduce your intake.

Intelligently add or increase:

1. Fiber
2. Whole grains
3. Beans and legumes
4. Nuts and seeds
5. Fresh fruits and fresh fruit juices
6. Fresh vegetables and fresh vegetable juices
7. Fish and white meat
8. Vitamin and mineral supplements (Vitamins A, C, E, and selenium especially)
9. Herbs and herb teas

I suggest you decrease your caloric intake if you are overweight. The benefits of proper nutrition are much broader than you might realize. Consider these points:

1. Proper nutrition will directly reduce stress, and reduced stress allows your immune system to function properly (which is your goal). While this has been a matter of speculation in the past, I know of at least one study (unpublished, by Dr. Seyta Brown) which shows that the immune system is directly stimulated by nutrition. In addition, a recent Boston study of people over

65 has shown that for them, a diet high in beta carotene reduces the risk of cancer, again highlighting the relationship between diet and the immune system.

2.   Good nutrition increases energy, and people with cancer need energy to get well and stay well. One symptom of cancer is a feeling of fatigue, so it is especially important to get energy from every available source. Fresh food and food supplements are simple, easy to get, and easy to take.

3.   Good nutrition keeps your emotions on an even keel. Since almost all people with cancer suffer depression, often without realizing it, a diet high in B vitamins is essential. At one point I ran out of a niacin supplement and went without it for a few weeks. I slipped gradually into depression, not realizing it until I started the niacin again and actually felt the cloud lift.

Improper nutrition can result in erratic behavior, not only in hyperactive children, who dramatically calm down when sugar and specific food additives are removed from their diets, but in everyone.

4.   Your body is strengthened by proper nutrition. Truly, we are what we eat. The food we eat forms the cells in our body, and a nourished body is a healthy body.

5.   Proper nutrition is a source of nurturance, a way of caring for your body. It is something that soothes you and tells your physical self that you care for it. Eat fresh food, take time, eat in a quiet, peaceful atmosphere, and choose the foods you enjoy so meals can be a source of relaxation and pleasure.

6.   "The mind is strengthened by the discipline we exercise over a selected diet," says Marcus Bach, a seventy-five-year-old author of twenty books who has studied lifestyle and nutrition all over the world. Positive in his outlook and full of vitality, he has told me that he knows of no better way to strengthen the mind than to exercise discipline over what you eat.

Your brain is an organ and is like other organs in the body, and the food you provide it improves the function. What and how you think affects your feelings: what and how you feel affects your body: what and how your body feels affects your mind—it is a closed circle.

Excuses, Excuses

If you don't nourish yourself properly look at your reasons for not paying attention to a healthy diet.

1. It's too difficult, I haven't got the willpower.
2. I don't really believe diet can influence the state of my cancer.
3. The doctor (authority) didn't say anything about diet.
4. The struggle is not worth it.
5. I'd sooner die than reduce or give up alcohol, rich food, caffeine . . . (name your poison).
6. I feel sick when I eat poorly, but I'm too sick to change.

These are just a few common excuses. What are your stoppers?

Once you can clearly identify them, then you have a choice. You can give them up and do something, or keep the stoppers and do nothing. It's always your choice. For me, doing something, anything, that has even the slimmest chance of helping is my choice.

Gregory Bateson, a Cambridge anthropologist, speaks of optimum value:

More is always better than less—that's the credo of greed. But it is *never* true biologically. There is always an optimum value beyond which anything is toxic, no matter what—oxygen, sleep, psychotherapy, and exercise. In both of these areas there is a tendency either to not do, or to overdo. You need to find a balance, an optimum, and it will be different for each person.

So these suggestions about food and nutrition are only a general guide. The specific diet will be your own. When you become aware of your body, it tells you what is right for you.

Awareness Helps

To become aware of what and why you eat, here is a technique that might help. Keeping a record of what goes on, happenings or your thoughts and feelings, is always a good idea for sorting things out, especially in times of crisis and stress. Try a modified form of journal-writing when you start, writing only about your diet in a journal. One way to look objectively at what goes into your body is to record it, so every day keep a record of everything you put into your mouth and swallow, and do it for a week—or two. Do it without trying to change your diet, just to get a picture of what you usually eat.

When you have a compelling desire or urge, your mind will often find or invent a reason to act on it. Recording these urges helps you become aware of rationalizations, and most of us rationalize a lot about food. Also, most of us have a genuine tendency toward wishful thinking, which is another way we deceive ourselves about what, when, and why we eat. We have sloppy food memories so what we eat and what we think we have eaten are quite often different.

Once you have the picture, read an article or a book (and I've listed some useful ones at the end of this chapter) and decide what things you might do to change the picture for the better. A move to better nutrition is one of the important life-style changes you can make.

I find it useful, too, to see diet in a broader sense—to keep in mind a Hindu belief that everything is food. They believe we feed not only on a vegetarian or nonvegetarian diet, but on all sound and light vibrations, on all the impressions we experience each day, on colors, on rhythms, on music, on our own beliefs, and on the beliefs of people we come in contact with. To swallow a daily dose of negative emotions is as destructive as a diet of junk food.

Not only the food I eat and the air I breathe, but everything I surround myself with each day make up the diet which I feed myself.

Exercise

There are few people now who would disagree that exercise is a factor in reducing stress. Hans Selye, the pioneer in stress research, found that chronic stress suppresses the immune system, your great ally against illness, and against cancer. Exercise also releases chemicals into the body that lift depression, the cancer patient's familiar companion.

The benefits of a regular exercise program in staying well are documented and described everywhere in this age of fitness. For those who have to get well first, and then stay that way, here are some of the most important benefits:

1. Exercise is an excellent form of relaxation. Basil A. Stoll, a consulting physician to the oncology and radiotherapy departments at St. Thomas Hospital in London, states:

    Training in relaxation can produce calmness, thereby reducing uncertainty. The rationale for this is that the secretion of stress hormones is thereby decreased and this may possibly result in a beneficial effect on the endocrine and immunological defense.

Uncertainty is something all cancer patients experience; it's inherent in the nature of the disease. For me, when I am tense and "uptight," nothing is more effective than to run off my tension. It not only relaxes my physical body, but also relaxes my mind, where the tension originates.

A neurotransmitter, seratonin, has been found to be helpful in easing stress and inducing calm sleep. Scientists theorize that seratonin may be boosted by exercise. They already know that another neurotransmitter that curbs depression, norepenephrine, is also boosted by exercise. And you get a natural "high" from endorphins released during exercise.

2. Regular exercise provides direct psychological benefits: You feel good afterward, and you have a sense of accomplishment because you have done the exercise. You increase your self-esteem and self-worth and this is essential to fighting cancer, as LeShan has pointed out. Among the people who come to the Hope program, it is obvious that those who exercise are the most positive, feel best about themselves, and are most active in fighting their cancer.

3. Regular exercise not only strengthens the body but also strengthens the mind. A strong mind will strengthen your body and your spirit. Dr. Roberto Assagioli, in *Act of Will*, speaks of the importance of physical exercise as an aid to strengthening the will.

4. Exercise done regularly will help you become more aware of and more in touch with your body. It is important to know and trust your body in order to judge the effectiveness of the program you are undertaking. Cancer patients are often out of touch with their bodies, and exercise is one of the best ways of changing this.

5. It is more effective to break depression with exercise than with drugs. There are very few cancer patients who don't experience depression, even though it is sometimes masked. Some doctors and researchers now

have evidence that emotional depression actually depresses the body's immune system. The times I feel the worst and am most reluctant to drag myself out to exercise are the times I most need it and most benefit by it. George Sheehan, one of North America's best-known addicted runners, expresses this "down" state in this way: "When I am ill I become a skeptic. What has hitherto been a certainty becomes perhaps; what was perhaps becomes maybe; and what was maybe becomes probably not."

The importance of exercising in spite of, and in fact for relief of, that "down" feeling is attested to by Dr. Robert Brown, a professor at the University of Virginia. He studied the effects of exercise on depression and found that in one group of new joggers, 38 percent reported depression before they began, while none of the joggers reported depression after eight weeks on a regular running program. It is known that aerobic exercise stimulates the production of norepinephrine, a neurotransmitter in the brain that is associated with good moods.

6. Exercise provides oxygen to your body, and sick bodies have reduced oxygenation. Breathing exercises are useful in increasing oxygenation. I became serious about exercise when I was told the brain needs and uses twenty times more oxygen than the rest of the body, so even in my worst state of paralysis, I exercised as much as I could.

7. Regular exercise tends to raise the pain threshold, according to experts on pain control. There is a tendency for cancer patients to baby themselves when it comes to exercise and to not exercise because it is tough when you're feeling sick. Illness doesn't make exercise any less important. Healthy parts of your body that are not moved deteriorate and stiffen, which can create or further increase pain.

Excuses Again

Here are some great excuses for not exercising, including some I've used myself on occasion:

1. I am too ill and exhausted.
2. I don't have enough time.
3. My doctor didn't tell me to exercise.
4. I try, but can't stick to it.
5. I'm not convinced exercise will help.
6. I'd rather die than exercise.

When I started a regular exercise program, I began with walking, progressed to a quarter-mile jog, then gradually increased to three or four miles at least five or six times per week. Because I increased it gradually, only once did I have an injury. I now supplement running with racquetball, swimming, and stretching exercises. It was a tremendous effort when I started. I'd put on my jogging shoes, then walk around the house for a half hour trying to psyche myself up, but gradually it has become pleasurable and now I find myself looking forward to it.

Some Hints

Here are some ways to ease yourself into exercise. Start with exercise that is easy and pleasant for you. If you don't enjoy it, you probably won't do it. Remember that it will be easier after one or two weeks, especially when you start feeling the benefits. Some say that you can become addicted to the endorphins your body produces. Best of all, get someone to do it with you. It's good company, and one of you will get the other going when you have a temporary lapse of will.

The form of exercise is your choice. Walking is considered one of the best; it is easy and inexpensive. Other more vigorous forms that also have an aerobic benefit are swimming, jogging, and cycling. Dancing, sex, yoga, and stretching are also good. Whatever you do, choose something you like, do it regularly, find someone to do it with, and start looking forward to it. It can be the most enjoyable medicine you take.

Support

Sidney Jourard speaks of self-disclosure as a powerful healer and my experience supports this assertion. There are very few events in my life that are not enhanced by sharing, and this is especially true of emotional experience. In times of crisis, this is doubly true.

People with cancer and those close to them experience intense emotions such as fear, anger, frustration, self-pity, victimization, and loss of control. The cancer patient usually won't communicate these emotions for a number of reasons, and two of the most common reasons are denial and protection. The first one, denial, goes like this: "If I don't talk about these feelings, they don't exist—or they'll go away." The second "protects" the family and friends: "It's bad enough I have this disease whose name we hardly dare mention, but to let them know how frightened and helpless I feel would be too much. I won't upset them anymore." Cancer patients are sickeningly stoic.

The family, as well, goes through the same process, sparing the patient the "burden" of their feelings. So communication stays on the level of clichés and niceties, and no one ever talks about what's really happening. Sandy, a friend, tells me that in the years of her father's illness no one ever said the word "cancer" in his presence. When everyone withdraws, then the person with cancer feels isolated, an unhealthy state for even a well person. A warm, close relationship is one of the strongest motivators to live.

The ideal would be to have a support system, and the open communication that is an integral part of it, within an existing relationship, within the family. However, because of the intensity of the emotion, the complex issues, and accumulated past history in a family, the ideal is not always possible. Simonton believes a support group to be one of the six requisites to getting well, and he strongly suggests that the support person or group be from outside the family.

So what does this support have to be or do? Nothing very complex, really.

Since one of the best ways to diffuse emotion is to "talk it out," all a good support person has to do is be there and listen. For me, the most honest communication is when I can relate what's going on with me without fear of being judged, criticized, or laughed at. When I can trust in that way, I can let go of the emotions that are pumping all that adrenaline into my system. When I share my fears with someone who can say, "Yes, I've been afraid myself," I feel closer and less isolated. I don't need advice, just understanding. A good listener doesn't have to know *why* I'm afraid, just that I *am* afraid; not *why* I feel hopeless, but just that I do feel that way. Somehow I feel less afraid and less hopeless just by talking about it.

Of course, the *best* listeners are those who understand because they have felt afraid or hopeless themselves. And the very best is the fellow cancer patient who has had the feelings and also experienced the "why's" of the alienation, the hopelessness, the nausea, the fatigue, the despair, and the panic of recurrence—and does not have to analyze why. And the ideal listener is the one who will also confront you about your apathy, blaming, and self-pity when he hears it. It was out of my own need for all this that I founded Hope.

Like improving your diet and starting an exercise program, getting a support person or group involves your own choice and initiative, although I admit it does take a little more psychological energy.

Because it takes energy and sometimes a little time, be wary of taking for your support a person who comes along to "rescue" you. You do not need someone who wants to "save" you (for their own need fulfillment, usually). You do not need someone to tell you it will be all right (when they don't know a damned thing about it). You don't need someone to tell you that you shouldn't worry, be afraid, be depressed, or whatever (when you bloody well do). What you need is someone to be there in this thing with you and listen. So thank the rescuers, and take some care in looking for some *real* support.

The easiest route is to find and join a group that already exists. The trust, understanding, and combined knowledge of a group is indescribable and invaluable. An alternative is to start a group of your own, which takes commitment and energy but gives you a goal—another requisite for recovery and health *if* the reason for starting is that it is for you; that is, if your motive is to start the group to meet *your* needs. Remember, the typical cancer patient has a history of doing things for others. Your goal, to be healthy, must be selfish, must be aimed at helping yourself.

The third alternative is to find some one person whom you feel you can trust and who is willing to listen. It might be as hard as directly asking someone—and maybe you would rather die than ask; it's your choice. It might be as simple as saying to a regular in a clinic or waiting room, "Do I look as tired as I feel?" or "I get scared every time I come here," and waiting to see if there is a response. Who knows what could develop? Self-disclosure can be hard but it is an amazingly powerful contact.

However you do it, when you have cancer, it is crucial to find and use a support system. As Carl Simonton once said, "Certainly there is pain in honesty, but in our experience it is minor compared with the pain of inevitable distance and isolation that occurs when someone cannot be himself."

Suggested Reading

Diet

Adams and Murray, *Body, Mind, and the B Vitamins*
Kirshman, *The Nutritional Almanac*
Passwater, *Cancer and Its Nutritional Therapies*

Exercise

Bach, *The Power of Total Living*
Sheehan, *Running and Being: The Total Experience*

People can be divided into three groups: those who make things happen, those who watch things happen, and those who wonder what happened.

John W. Newbern

13

One Good Thing After Another

IF 1982 WAS ABOUT STRUG-
gling with recurrence and with money, 1983 was about
struggling with the book, broadening my focus, and working
with Hope.

With my health back, I felt I was riding an exponential
curve. It was a very good year, the seventh year since my
divorce, and I had been telling myself over and over if I
could live seven years from 1975, I would make it. I know
our bodies regenerate their cells over a seven-year cycle, so
I felt I was giving myself a sound message. At home I had
fewer responsibilities. After having all the kids for two and a
half years, now only Doug was at home. Bub and Del were
going to college and living together on their own, and Sherry
was living on her own too. I had rented out the suite in my
house and also a couple of spare rooms. My relationship
with Doris was much less painful. We saw each other on
birthdays and other family occasions, and we talked on the
phone once in a while.

Money was still a concern. The Hope groups covered only
their overhead with a little left over for advertising. I
received no salary but I was spending all my time counseling and visiting hospitals. The fees were (and still are) low,
and follow-up sessions were free.

My journal used to be totally preoccupied with cancer and
health and the frustrations of writing the book. One journal
entry reads, "I feel that trying to write this book means
going through almost the same process as trying to get
well." I had 244 typewritten pages that looked great to me
one day and like garbage the next.

Of course, I had to have a dream about the book. It was
about writing a novel. At the time I thought, "I never read

novels and I'm not even interested in novels," but I recorded
the dream anyway, and when I read it a few weeks later, it
made sense. I was going to write something *novel,* something different. That was a heartening thought as I worked
to put the book into its final form.

But my journals were changing. Now they were records of
what I had found out, seminars I had attended, books I had
read, plans I was making. I wrote about the people in the
group. They were triggering so many of my past experiences
that I started to appreciate what *I* had gone through as I saw
them struggling with the same things. I spent a lot of the
year searching for ways to help them to help themselves
while knowing that ultimately they were the only ones who
could do it.

I found out about alternative health programs from people
who had been to them: the Neiper Clinic in Hanover,
Germany, where Dr. Hans Neiper uses beta carotene and
minerals and other supplements as well as chemotherapy;
the Janker Clinic in Bonn, where patients are treated with
combinations of chemotherapy, radiation, megavitamins,
minerals, enzymes, and immune stimulants under the direction of Dr. Wolfgang Scheef; the Lucas Clinic in Arlesheim,
Switzerland, with a program based on the Steiner program
and Iscador mistletoe, directed by Dr. Rita Le Roi; and the
Bristol Cancer Self-Help Center in Bristol, England, with a
truly holistic program centering on a raw food diet, Bach
Flower Remedies, biofeedback, and meditation. I spoke to
Dr. Lawrence Burton, whose clinic in the Bahamas is now
closed, and I spent a day in Menlo Park, California, looking
at the Creighton program, which is similar to the Simonton
program.

Almost all of them aimed to improve the body's immunological system, a different approach from surgery,
radiation, and chemotherapy, which are all invasive proce-
dures that further attack the body. My dominant question
was, "How can I and others get rid of cancer?" I read and
listened to immunologists, physicists, theologians, and phi-

losophers, and broadened my focus to include things not specifically related to health. I attended lectures on different mind-control techniques. During a process in one of them, I had a very detailed image of myself conducting a health seminar in Mazatlan with a group of fifteen cancer patients and I was staying at the La Siesta Hotel. Three months later, in February, I did just that.

The trip to Mazatlan was part of improving our lives and having some fun together. Working now with thirty-five to forty people on an ongoing basis, we were having about ten weekend workshops a year. Almost all the participants were considered terminal, and in the fall, three people died in ten days, which was particularly hard. Again I wondered whether I should be doing this. Was I misleading everyone, including myself, by putting out false hopes? But I was able to put the doubts aside. I stopped questioning the program, because although it was small, it was growing and I had made a commitment.

The people coming to the workshops were a diverse group. It included men and women, some of them as young as fourteen, some over seventy, from all walks of life. Some came back for the follow-up nights held once every two weeks, and they gradually built up a trust so that they could really listen to us and then start talking about themselves. It often took a while before they could trust what was going on because we were looking at cancer in a totally different way. But the people who continued became very close, and many are still part of the group now, four years later.

That year we had the first Hope article published in a major newspaper and I spent more time on promotion. I didn't know much about it but I was learning. By 1984 our 400 to 500 calls a year had grown to around 2,000. Not everyone joined a group but we were providing them with a service by answering their questions.

There were comparatively few personal notations in my journals in 1983, but one entry in March was, "Cancer is, but I am. I am far more than my cancer."

My journals reflect a shift in focus as I move from internalizing my feelings to being more expressive of them. Through 1983 and 1984, they describe my attempts to review my experiences for the sake of others who might benefit from them. This new externalization is embodied in the formation of the Hope network and the writing of this book.

If I were asked to briefly sum up what I have learned, to dispense it as advice, I'd say, "Avoid the pitfalls"—and these are the pitfalls as I see them:

1. Thinking there's one "magic pill" and, when something doesn't work, throwing it out. Cancer is multifactorial so it must be treated in a multifactoral way. You must put a number of things together to effect a cure and to stay well.
2. Not trusting yourself, being unduly influenced by others, and being rushed to decide on the course of treatment. Take your time to find out all you can and trust your own informed decision. People who actively engage in their own treatment do better.
3. Isolating the cancer from the rest of your life, not seeing it as related. You must see cancer as a message about your life and the message is: something has to change.
4. Doubting that you can ever get well. Others often support you implicitly in this—so stay away from them. Surround yourself with people who know you can do it.
5. Feeling there is really nothing you can do—thinking something esoteric has to happen to you before you can get well. Read *Getting Well Again*. Read *this* book again. Read other books about survivors. Know that you can improve the quality of your life and extend it.
6. Staying with the wrong doctor, and placing your faith in a doctor because he *is* a doctor. Find a doctor who will act as an expert consultant. Find one who will help and support you in the choices you make together.
7. Feeling guilty and blaming yourself for the disruption in

family life and for your inability to continue working outside your home, to cook the meals (or both), to have energy to do extra things. Stay focused on your objective, which is to make yourself well, or you won't be around at all to do those other things.

8. Ignoring your own needs, being stoic. Not asking for what you want. Find someone to share your feelings with, and go for something you want for a change. Holding your feelings in and always meeting others' needs helped make you sick to begin with.

9. Allowing yourself to drift through until the panic stage. "We got it all" comes with a limited guarantee. Denying what's happening keeps you from deep psychological pain but it also keeps you from doing what you have to do to stay healthy.

Make a commitment to live. Things will change radically once you make this commitment. In the words of Goethe:

Until one is committed, there is hesitancy, the chance to draw back, always ineffectiveness, concerning all acts of initiative (and creation). There is one elementary truth, the ignoring of which kills countless ideas and splendid plans; that the moment one commits oneself then Providence moves too. All sorts of things occur to help one that would never otherwise have occurred. A whole stream of events issues from the decision, raising in one's favor all manner of unforeseen incidents and material assistance which no man could have dreamed would come his way. Whatever you can do or dream you can, begin it. Boldness has genius, power, and magic in it. Begin it now.

14

Excerpts from My Journal

After a workshop on journal writing in 1974, I started what I thought would be a few weeks of journal writing and I have never stopped.

I write almost daily, sometimes a few lines, sometimes a few pages. Writing in my journal has become a useful and necessary part of my life. During times of intense emotional turmoil, when I have no one to talk to I can at least write in my journal and it provides some relief. I also learn from it. It helps me to clarify what I am going through, and as I look back, I can see how I have moved and grown. My journals show how, over the past ten years, with all my wild swings up and down, I have always come back to near-center, and that has saved me. Here are some excerpts from my journals.

Early 1976 [before diagnosed as having cancer]—I have this incredible yearning for Doris, my family, a home and some love. I know the cause of suffering is craving, but knowing this doesn't stop it. On the verge of despair again. The nights are the worst.

My balance is not good and I hate my clumsiness. I can't look anyone in the eye and nobody gives a shit what happens to me.

Good Friday—Feel like I'm the one being crucified. Kids are with Doris and I'm alone with my limping leg in this dark little basement suite.

Easter Sunday—Starved for love. I'm so weak—what's the use. I sit and stare at the wall for hours. Steve comes by to say hello and cheer me up. He and Tonia are good people and I try to be friendly but I feel so empty. I've got nothing to give. I envy their caring relationship.

Met with the fire adjuster and always feel ripped off by him. I must get some energy to fight back or I'll end up with nothing. If he finds out I'm in psych hospital and very depressed, he'll really screw me.

May 5—The divorce papers are signed. I say nothing to Doris and she says little to me. My right hand shakes so much it is almost impossible to write.

I spend too much time sitting in cafes and drinking coffee and feeling sorry for myself.

Del, I cried over your letter. It was the first time I felt loved for so long. I read it over and over.

(I write to Doris at Cortes Island exactly one year after she leaves.) Doris, you must be very pleased to be divorced from a cripple. I hope you and Leon fuck yourselves to death. What a wonderful best friend Leon turned out to be. God, I hate what you're doing but I can't get rid of my love for you.

After going out together for six months, Ann tells me she just wants to be friends and wants no sex. I expected it but it still hurts. I'm sure neither she or any other woman wants to be with a depressed cripple!! The only thing I can count on a woman for is hurt.

October 11—Thanksgiving Day. Another typical, rotten holiday. I don't feel thankful about anything!

November 8—Drove Sheila home from class last night—feel attracted to her and also sexually frustrated. I don't say anything. I know she's not interested in me.

December 15—I dread another Christmas by myself.

January 1, 1977 (Esalen Institute, Big Sur, California)—Looking for ways to stop this psychological paralysis.

January 14 (Monterey, California)—Ten expensive acupuncture treatments, only temporary relief.

February 5 (San Francisco)—Complete a four-day EST program.

Dragging my heavy right leg takes so much energy, which really wears me down. Writing (the physical act) has never been so difficult.

February 25 (Sacramento)—Saw Ann Armstrong, a psychic. She tells me about my family, etc. I'm impressed. No clues as to what's wrong with me. Suggests B vitamins.

I dream of being rejected by Doris.

March—Take some fucking <u>risks</u>, Claude!

April—I'm starting regular bioenergetic sessions to try to get the life back into my right side. Arm and leg still deteriorating. God, what is happening to me; I'm out on a limb and can't get down.

I so badly need to be held and loved. Jackie is my best support right now—she's warm and concerned but suicide thoughts still with me every day.

April—I'm diagnosed as having an inoperable brain tumor—what a relief.

May 14—Feel like walking in front of a car. Always by myself. NO LOVE. Absolutely no control over my life.

Bought an old house two weeks after being diagnosed with a tumor. I must be crazy.

I'm having a hard time figuring out what is real and what is
unreal.

I hear a strong nurturing relationship is important to
reduce stress. I haven't got one and I don't know how to
get one. I keep thinking about Doris and Leon having sex.
I feel intense jealousy much of the time.

June 9—The hatred in me right now is overwhelming. Not
one damn person cares. If I don't act correctly, everyone
withdraws. Withdrawal is the greatest punishment there
is.

June 24—I'm so frustrated with dragging my body around.
How can I love this fucking mess of a body—how can I
love this dangling piece of flesh I call my right hand? I
hate myself, I hate everything.

July—A therapist tells me to substitute a positive image in
place of Doris. I try, it doesn't work.

August—Rita phoned to suggest we go for coffee. She's got
even more problems than I have.

August—A relationship is developing with Robyn. When I go
out with her I can forget about Doris. Robyn confronts me
and I like it. She feels free to touch my right hand as does
Rosemary who massages it for me.

September 1—Doris comes over to the house and in less than
5 minutes we're screaming and fighting. She keeps hitting
me—but it's better than nothing.

October 1—Today I was so down. Doug put his arms around
me and gave me a hug. I hid my tears.

I spend so much time daydreaming and so little time
doing.

I've heard it's only when you're vulnerable that you can fully experience life. Well I'm vulnerable and I hate it. I hate the pain.

December 2—Robyn keeps sending me cards and love notes . . .

Sherry has taken over as the mother in the house.

Things are so rotten I just want to pack up and leave forever. I will write a book about rejection.

February 1978—Struggling with exercise—it took great effort to swim a half a length today.

March 27—Start of consulting job in Vernon. It helps allay my money worries.

I've tried visualizing the energy swirling through my right arm but I'm giving up after a week. Sometimes my arm is strong and sometimes it just dangles—I can't figure it out.

May 1—I've been on vitamins for some time and today I started on megavitamins.

June 12—I had another CAT scan. Dr. Griesdale's nurse reports the tumor is definitely larger. I feel more scared than ever—at least it distracts me from thinking about Doris.

June 22—The tumor is growing and no treatments are available. I'm reading *Spontaneous Regression of Cancer* by Boyd.

August 1 [Dr. Donald Stewart, my G.P., writes in my journal:]—That which you can conceive of, believe in and constantly expect for yourself, must become your experience.

I feel so bitchy and irritated lately and it all comes out at the kids.

August 15—Last night's dream suggests I don't have to be an M.D. to treat myself.

November 29—Keith died of a brain tumor. We never liked each other. His dying, about a week after being diagnosed, really upsets me. My headache has been going on for days.

December 15, 3 a.m.—Got up to change the sheets—they're wet with "fear sweat."

January 1979—Money anxieties distract me from Doris and my right side.

February 26—On my way to California to go to the "Death and Dying" Retreat. I may never have the experience of getting old.

March 18 (Yucca Valley, California)—[With great effort I wrote down a few gems during the one-week Death and Dying Retreat:]

You can't deal with truth with people who don't want the truth.

When you're full of knowing, it's impossible to hear.

April 10 (back in Vancouver)—I feel like crying all the time but never do. The constant feeling that I don't matter to anyone keeps coming up.

July 1—Worried about money. I see myself sick and destitute on skid road. My negative images are so powerful.

Realize I have an insurance policy and could get a small disability pension for a maximum of two years but the insurance company won't pay. I'm hiring a lawyer.

August 15—Will take the consulting job in Kelowna. It's out of town and could be difficult.

Doris was the one who ended the relationship, but I feel pressure from the kids, especially Sherry, to maintain it. Sherry wants so badly for us to get back together.

My body is so crippled. I had no idea of how sick I could be. I don't know if it's gone too far to beat it. Every cell in my body feels weak and tired. Thinking of putting an ad in the newspaper saying "willing to pay handsomely for advice on how I can get away from myself."

Today I wrote a long poem titled "If I Had a Million Dollars" and realized it wouldn't be of much use to me. It wouldn't buy love or health and it certainly wouldn't pay anybody to die for me. Right now I don't feel ready to die. There are too many things to do. Ha! It's the height of egotism to think I have control over my death when I can't even control my life.

December 20, 1979 [From a long letter I never sent:]—Dear Mom and Dad, You know I realize now when confronting death that love is the only thing that really matters and everything else is really insignificant and unimportant. I know that God is love in the highest form but this still feels like a concept to me rather than an experience. Do you love me? Does anybody love me?

February 6, 1980 (back from the Philippines)—At the symphony, all I can think of is how tired the conductor's arm must feel. I have to close my eyes. It is the only way to hear the music, otherwise all I can think about is my own heavy arm.

(I try to meditate and relax but I can't and instead I write.) Panic spreads over my body as I try to relax, my mind refuses to focus on anything. I struggle desperately in my silence, my voice is blocked by fears, no one can hear and I feel completely isolated.

March 12—Saw Robyn yesterday evening. She makes me feel good and powerful. When she's turned on to me I feel sexually desirable and have greater confidence in myself. Her beauty and intensity feel good. Then her fear comes up that I'll die and she becomes cold and withdrawn, just another person who's given up on me. My body is so crippled and awkward it's embarrassing to sleep with her.

March 20 [This page is ripped by my pen]—It's rotten being a cripple and having no energy!! [In small letters at the bottom of the page:] My intent will be realized—what do you really intend, Claude?

April 8—The CAT scan shows the tumor is still there. I'm disappointed and angry at those damned psychic healers. I give up!

April 10—Hope back again today. The psychic healers' care, concern, and energy have healed my spiritual body and I know the physical healing will follow.

I need less drama in my life and more reality.

Once again a long talk with Doris about my fears etc., and she seems to make everything so right.

June—Not asking for help may be the biggest barrier I have to getting well.

August 15—Many things lately move me to tears. Feel my chances are slim and yet today I start out writing the introduction and outline of the book. I need to write and to enroll in a writing class.

September 10—I sit for hours watching the tide wash up against this big log. As I move I realize I've also caused Doris great pain. I experience some of the sorrow she must have gone through.

September 12—First day of radiation.

October 3—Great to get up feeling so positive about the day and hopeful about the radiation treatment; I'm tired but optimistic.

End of October—I feel great anxiety about getting better. Things are going too well. I crave salt and sweets. I think the radiation has dulled my sense buds and I need more intense tastes.

Judy LaMarsh died yesterday of pancreatic cancer. The newspapers always have stories about people dying of cancer.

February 23, 1981—Today I visited Bob in Lion's Gate Hospital. [Bob has been a member of Hope for 9 months.] He's dying and knows it. He keeps saying, "I got smart too late." My feelings are strong: anger, fright, sadness, and the feeling I hate most, helplessness.

June—Jane, an R.N. at the Cancer Clinic, and I go out. I enjoy her company. We never talk about cancer.

June 22—Mark died today. [Mark is a Hope member.] He was peaceful. I didn't feel close but was very moved by him.

July 22—Fight with Doris, which I started as a result of feeling rejected, ignored, and unimportant.

September 28—Some days I feel like giving up.

I really like all the people in Hope. Eddie was so funny last night, he had everyone in stitches.

November 21 (Healing Brain Seminar, Seattle)—What an array of M.D.'s and Ph.D.'s. I'm taking pages and pages of notes to share with Hope members. What a joy to write so easily with my right hand again.

January 5, 1982—(It's 10:30 p.m. and the last person from Hope group meeting has left. I sit writing by the fire.) The personal power each of us has is amazing. Writing a book for people with cancer is my definite goal this year.

February—I jogged four miles for the first time.

There was a lot of blaming of doctors in the Hope group tonight. I used to try and stop it. Now I believe it is a stage we all must go through, but continued blaming stops us from helping ourselves. I remember a therapist telling me, "Lucky is the man that has no scapegoats." When I figured out what this meant, I was pissed off, as I often am when something hits the mark.

March—Today I re-read my recent journals—far less crazy emotions going on now. They are mostly about cancer patients in Hope, cancer books, and health seminars.

March 12—Anxiety about going to Hawaii with Flo-May. Flo-May, I'm attracted to your sensitivity and afraid of your emotional pain. You have such a struggle with your life and sometimes it deflects on me.

April 12—On a Hotline radio phone-in program for the first time. It was easier than I expected, much easier than the first time on television when the interviewer's first question was, "Are you a quack?"

May 29 [Dr. Marcus Bach speaks at Unity Church, Vancouver]—Dr. Bach gives me a new perspective on body, mind, and spirit. He says, "If you <u>really</u> believe in something you will do it." New Hope members seem to find it easy to agree and hard to DO.

If you're considered terminal and want to get well, you've got to have a real hunger for life. [I often write messages to myself.]

June 1—Why do I continue with the Hope program? Tonight I'm in despair about the session. Many people coming only as a "last-ditch" effort are far too sick to concentrate. Some don't seem to have a commitment to living. They want a magic bullet. They feel no power in themselves to help themselves. I'm tired of it all. What's the use?

October 2—Today after the Hope group I became aware of my transition from cancer patient to cancer therapist. Moyra and I are noticing not only cancer personality traits but specific traits and behaviors that relate to different <u>types</u> of cancer.

November—Betty called to tell me her cancer had spread to her throat. Right now I feel very down. There is little joy in my life. I have a strong image that my depression, frustration, and worry are like water and fertilizer for my tumor.

November 5—Today Sherry is 21 and Del is 20. They're grown up, and I'm proud of their independence.

I have given up coffee at least a dozen times. I started drinking it again today.

April 1983—Today I met Ethel, who, after three years in a wheelchair, is walking as a result of her treatment in the Janker Clinic in Germany.

Christmas—Family dinner with Doris and the kids—better than usual.

December 26—Spent this wonderful sunny day with Moyra, walking around Stanley Park. She has become a co-leader in Hope and I very much respect her sensitivity and perceptions. I am learning from her.

January 1, 1984—Ended 1983 with many good things happening but I am still feeling unsuccessful. The Cancer Clinic will not recognize the Hope program. The officials believe that emotional support and attitude play no part in getting well. The greater opposition I get, the more I resolve to go on. When cancer treatment is a monopoly, the patients suffer.

January 7—The press talks negatively about Salvador Dali being obsessed about his own death. Why shouldn't he be? It's the single most important event in his life.

January 16—6:30 a.m. off to Mazatlan for two weeks (with 15 members of Hope).

January 17 (Mazatlan)—Doris Currie, who came to Hope with breast cancer that had spread to her bones and spine, couldn't sit for more than 15 minutes in 1982. Today she went up 200 feet on a parachute pulled behind a speed boat. We all took pictures.

March 5—My whole life is about cancer. I need a change.

March 19 [Running a "Just for the Health of It" week-long seminar at Cortes for people who are healthy.]—This is the third day. Some of these healthy people have problems that seem more terrible than those we with cancer have. Is anyone without pain?

March—Doug is 19 now and the only one left at home. Why can't we talk more? There used to be a lot of love between us and now there is nothing. We eat together and that's all. Today I blew up and yelled at him. He stood up to me at the time and then withdrew even further. I try hard to ignore the constant stress our coldness is causing me. I stress myself even further by drinking too much coffee.

June—Today Dr. Stewart showed me the results of my regular lab tests and we discuss them. The hemoglobin, triglycerine, and cholesterol levels were all good—better than nine months previous.

July 24—Doug tells me he is going to move out. I don't feel at all upset, as things are good between us again. Doug, Bub, Del, and Sherry have been supportive in so many ways in the past few years but it will be wonderful to be completely on my own in my house.

August 15—A General Practitioner phones me to consult about a person with cancer. The first time!

September 9—I complain to a friend about the establishment and all health professionals being closed to anything new. His response, "Shake the status quo until it rattles." This is the way I feel right now but it isn't the answer. I want to work *with* the establishment, not against it.

September 25 (Toronto)—Nice visit with Laurian. Looking forward to two weeks in this exciting city.

Moyra and I have been invited by Dr. Alastair J. Cunningham to lead an evening seminar at the Ontario Cancer Society offices.

December 3—A doctor on a CBC program claims that cancer chemotherapy is the biggest fraud going. He says chemotherapy is used now routinely on breast, colon, and lung cancer as prophylactic therapy. I can't believe I have heard him correctly and write for the transcript.

Moyra and I go to Cortes Island over the holidays and resolve not to talk about cancer. We don't.

How to Write a Book

WHEN YOU ARE PHYSICALLY unable to write, you decide to write a book. You make it a goal and think about it, talk about it, and most important, scrawl in your journal every day the things you want to remember. Eventually you start writing a great stream of consciousness manuscript, have it typed (264 pages double-spaced), and duplicated, and give it to three people to read. One reads it and gives you feedback, one reads it and gets angry, and one doesn't read it at all. You don't know which depresses you most. You wait a year. You show it to a friend who is a writer. You get feedback, get depressed, and wait another ten months. Then you and the writer friend take the manuscript to Hawaii. Three weeks of sun, water, fresh air, and twelve-hour workdays later, you have a book.

Selected Reading

Achterberg, Jeanne, and G. Frank Lawlis. *Imagery of Disease: An Evaluation Tool for Behavioral Medicine.* Champaign, Ill.: Institute for Personality and Ability Testing.

———, O. Carl Simonton, and Stephanie Matthews-Simonton, eds. *Stress, Psychological Factors and Cancer.* Fort Worth, Tex.: New Medicine Press, 1976.

Adams, Ruth, and Frank Murray. *Body, Mind, and the B Vitamins*, rev. New York: Larchmont, 1972.

Araneta, Antonio, and Jesus B. Lava, M.D. *Faith Healing and Psychic Surgery*, rev. Philippine Society for Psychical Research Foundation, 1983.

Assagioli, Roberto. *Act of Will.* New York: Penguin, 1974.

Bach, Marcus. *The Power of Total Living.* New York: Fawcett, Crest Books, 1978.

Bakan, David. *Disease, Pain, and Sacrifice: Toward a Psychology of Suffering.* Boston, Mass.: Beacon Press, 1971.

Benson, Herbert, and Miriam Z. Klipper. *The Relaxation Response.* New York: Avon, 1976.

Boyd, William. *Spontaneous Regression Of Cancer.* 1966 photocopy ed. spiral.

Brown, Barbara B. *Between Health and Illness: New Notions on Stress and the Nature of Well Being.* New York: Bantam, 1985.

———. *New Mind, New Body: Bio-feedback; New Directions for the Mind.* New York: Harper & Row, 1974.

Bry, Adelaide, and Marjorie Bair. *Visualization: Directing the Movies of Your Mind.* New York: Barnes & Noble, div. of Harper & Row, 1979.

Cantor, Robert C. *And a Time to Live: Toward Emotional Well-Being During the Crisis of Cancer.* New York: Harper & Row, 1980.

Cousins, Norman. *Anatomy of an Illness*. Toronto/New York: Bantam, 1981.

————. *The Healing Heart: Antidotes to Panic and Helplessness*. New York: Norton, 1983.

Fiore, Neil A. *The Road Back to Health: Coping with the Emotional Side of Cancer*. New York: Bantam, 1984.

Fox, Emmet. *The Sermon on the Mount*. New York: Harper & Row, 1934.

Frankl, Victor E. *Man's Search for Meaning*. New York: Pocket Books, div. of Simon & Schuster, 1980.

Gawain, Shakti. *Creative Visualization*. New York: Bantam, 1982.

Glassman, J. *The Cancer Survivors*. New York: Dial, 1983.

Goodfield, June. *The Siege of Cancer*. New York: Dell, 1975.

Hutschnecker, Arnold A. *The Will to Live*. New York: Cornerstone, div. of Simon & Schuster, 1982.

Israel, Lucien. *Conquering Cancer*. New York: Random House, 1978.

Jaffe, Dennis T. *Healing from Within*. New York: Knopf, 1980.

Joy, W. Brugh. *Joy's Way*. Los Angeles: Tarcher, 1979.

Jung, C.G. *Memories, Dreams, Reflections*. London: Collins and Routledge and Kegan Paul, 1963.

Kidman, Brenda. *A Gentle Way with Cancer*, rev. ed. London: Century, 1985.

King, Serge. *Imagineering for Health*. Wheaton, Ill.: Theosophical Publishing House, 1981.

Kirschmann, John D., and Lavon J. Dunne, eds. *Nutrition Almanac*, 2d ed. New York: McGraw-Hill, 1984.

Kothari, M.L., and L.A. Mehta. *Cancer: Myths and Realities of Cause and Cure*. Published simultaneously in Great Britain (London) and U.S.A. (Salem, N.H.): Marion Boyars Ltd., dist. by Scribner, 1979.

LeShan, Lawrence. *How to Meditate: A Guide to Self-Discovery*. New York: Bantam, 1975.

————. *The Mechanic and the Gardener*. New York: Holt, Rinehart and Winston, 1982.

————. *You Can Fight for Your Life: Emotional Factors in the Treatment of Cancer.* New York: M. Evans, 1977.

Lorenz, Frederick. *Cancer, A Mandate to Humanity.* Spring Valley, N.Y.: Mercury Press, 1982 (pamphlet).

Maltz, Maxwell. *Psychocybernetics.* Richmond Hill, Ont.: Simon & Schuster of Canada Ltd. 1971 (Originally published by Prentice-Hall, 1960).

McCamy, John C., and James Presley. *Human Life Styling.* New York: Harper & Row, 1977.

Meek, George W., ed. *Healers and the Healing Process.* Wheaton, Ill.: Theosophical Publishing House, 1977.

Naisbitt, John, ed. *Megatrends: Ten New Directions Transforming Our Lives.* New York: Warner Books, 1982.

Oyle, Irving. *New American Medicine Show.* Santa Cruz, Calif.: Unity Press, 1981.

Passwater, Richard A. *Cancer and Its Nutritional Therapies,* rev. ed. New Canaan, Conn.: Keats, 1983.

Pelletier, Kenneth R. *Mind as Healer, Mind as Slayer.* New York: Dell, 1977.

————. *Holistic Medicine.* New York: Dell, 1979.

Ponder, Catherine. *The Dynamic Laws of Healing.* Marina del Rey, Calif.: DeVorss, 1972.

Dass, Ram. *The Only Dance There Is.* New York: Anchor Press, Doubleday, 1974.

Seyle, Hans. *The Stress of Life.* New York: McGraw-Hill, 1978.

————. *Stress Without Distress.* Philadelphia/New York: Lippincott, 1975.

Shames, Richard, and Chuck Sterin. *Healing with Mind Power.* Emmaus, Penn.: Rodale Press, 1980.

Sheehan, George. *Running and Being: The Total Experience.* New York: Warner, 1978.

Simonton, O. Carl, Stephanie Matthews-Simonton, and James Creighton. *Getting Well Again: A Step-by-Step Self-Help Guide to Overcoming Cancer for Patients and Their Families.* Los Angeles: Tarcher, 1978.

Stoll, Basil A., ed. *Mind and Cancer Prognosis.* New York: Wiley, 1980.

Stone, Irwin. *The Healing Factor: Vitamin C Against Disease.* New York: Putnam, 1972.

Tillich, Paul. *The Courage to Be.* New Haven, Conn.: Yale University Press, 1952.

About the Authors

When he was diagnosed as having an inoperable brain tumor in 1977, CLAUDE DOSDALL had been a hospital administrator for sixteen years and was an elected town councilman. He spent several years attending lectures and seminars, meeting different specialists and researching various kinds of treatment for cancer. Then, in 1980, Mr. Dosdall founded Hope, a non-profit self-help support group for cancer patients and their families. Today he spends all his time directing Hope, facilitating groups and lecturing throughout western Canada. He is the father of four children and lives in Vancouver's Kitsilano district.

JOANNE BROATCH is a freelance editor and writer and a consultant in business writing. She is the author of several articles on education and health-related topics, and of the book, *Better Back, Better Body*. She lives in Vancouver.

SEAL BOOKS PRESENTS
THE CANADIAN MEDICAL LIBRARY

Seal Books is pleased to launch this valuable new series of comprehensive handbooks from the experts. Each book in the Canadian Medical Library will provide up-to-date medical information in easy-to-read reference form on everyday popular subjects.

Look for the first two volumes in this important addition to the Seal Books list.

HEART ATTACKS, HYPERTENSION AND HEART DRUGS
by Dr. Gabriel Khan

Dr. Khan is a renowned cardiologist, and this is his common-sense guide to a healthy heart. In addition to looking at risk factors, and the importance of fitness and a sensible diet, Dr. Khan provides a thorough review of the newest in heart drugs such as beta-blockers.

SURVIVING BREAST CANCER
by Carole Spearin McCauley

Ms. McCauley, once a science writer for the National Institute of Health, has assembled the latest facts about breast cancer in an effort to suppress the widespread fear spawned from ignorance. Readers will find comprehensive information about the necessity and advisability of mastectomies and as well this book offers many personal anecdotes and case histories.

SEAL BOOKS

Offers you a list of outstanding fiction, non-fiction and classics of Canadian literature in paperback by Canadian authors, available at all good bookstores throughout Canada.

THE BACK DOCTOR	Hamilton Hall
THE IVORY SWING	Janette Turner Hospital
NEVER CRY WOLF	Farley Mowat
THE KITE	W.O. Mitchell
BIRD IN THE HOUSE	Margaret Laurence
ANNE OF GREEN GABLES	Lucy Maud Montgomery
BEST CANADIAN SHORT STORIES	John Stevens, Ed.
LADY ORACLE	Margaret Atwood
AN INNOCENT MILLIONAIRE	Stephen Vizinczey
BORDERLINE	Janette Turner Hospital
AND NO BIRDS SANG	Farley Mowat
THE DANCE OF SHIVA	William Deverell
STONE ANGEL	Margaret Laurence
STRAIGHT FROM THE HEART	Jean Chretien
BLUEBEARD'S EGG	Margaret Atwood
JOSHUA THEN AND NOW	Mordecai Richler
MY DISCOVERY OF AMERICA	Farley Mowat
A CERTAIN MR. TAKAHASHI	Ann Ireland
THE CANADIAN ESTABLISHMENT	Peter C. Newman
A JEST OF GOD	Margaret Laurence
HOW I SPENT MY SUMMER HOLIDAYS	W.O. Mitchell
ANNE OF WINDY POPLARS	Lucy Maud Montgomery
SEA OF SLAUGHTER	Farley Mowat
THE HANDMAID'S TALE	Margaret Atwood
THE CANADIANS (seven volumes)	Robert E. Wall
JACOB TWO TWO MEETS THE HOODED FANG	Mordecai Richler
HEART OF A STRANGER	Margaret Laurence
THE DOG WHO WOULDN'T BE	Farley Mowat
WHO HAS SEEN THE WIND	W.O. Mitchell
THE ACQUISITORS	Peter C. Newman
LIFE BEFORE MAN	Margaret Atwood

The Mark of Canadian Bestsellers